THE PROGRAMME OF THE
N.S.D.A.P.

THE NATIONAL SOCIALIST GERMAN WORKER'S PARTY AND ITS GENERAL CONCEPTIONS

GOTTFRIED FEDER

WITH AN INTRODUCTION BY

ALEXANDER JACOB

First published Munich 1932
by Fritz Eher Verlag

The Programme of the N.S.D.A.P.
the National Socialist German Worker's Party
and Its General Conceptions

Gottfried Feder

With an Introduction by
Alexander Jacob

ISBN-13: 978-1-913176-57-0

All rights reserved. No part of this book may be reproduced in any form by any electronic or mechanical means including photocopying, recording, or information storage and retrieval without permission in writing from the publisher.

Sanctuary Press Ltd
71-75 Shelton Street
Covent Garden
London
WC2H 9JQ

www.sanctuarypress.com
Email: info@sanctuarypress.com

Contents

Introduction	1
The Rise of the N.S.D.A.P.	15
Preface	25
The Official Party Manifesto	27
1. The Policy of the N.S.D.A.P.	35
2. The 25 Points	43
3. The Basic Ideas	51
4. The Programme Requirements In Detail	65
5. What We Do Not Desire	99
6. Conclusion	101

Introduction

Gottfried Feder was born in 1883 in Würzburg and studied engineering at the Technical Universities in Munich, Berlin and Zurich. After the completion of his studies he set up a construction company of his own in 1908 under the aegis of Ackermann and Co. and undertook several projects in Bulgaria. From 1917 onwards he taught himself financial politics and economics and, in late 1918, not long after the proclamation of the Weimar Republic by Philipp Scheidemann in November of that year, Feder wrote a manifesto on usury[1] and sent it to the Kurt Eisner government, though he obtained no response. The Treaty of Versailles signed in June 1919 which determined Germany as solely responsible for the war and liable to reparations caused Feder to fear that Germany was now firmly in the hands of the international financiers. In September of that year, Feder established a militant league (Kampfbund) for the breaking of interest slavery and the nationalisation of the state bank. His anti-capitalism was bound also to racialism insofar as the international financiers were considered to be mostly Jews.

Feder's nationalist efforts drew him into a close alliance with the anti-Communist activist Anton Drexler (1884-1942) and Dietrich Eckart (1868-1923), the editor of the anti-Semitic journal Auf gut deutsch and later, of the National Socialist organ, Völkischer Beobachter. The three together formed, in January 1919, the Deutsche Arbeiter Partei (DAP).[2] Adolf Hitler joined the DAP in late September 1919 and soon emerged as the

---

1 *Manifest zur Brechung des Zinsknechtschaft des Geldes*, Diessen vor München: Joseph C. Huber, 1919; cf. *Manifesto for Breaking of the Financial Slavery to Interest*, tr. Alexander Jacob, London, Black House Publishing, 2015
2 Another major early member was Karl Harrer (1890-1926), who joined the party in March of 1919. Harrer, like Drexler, was a member of the occultist Thule society in Munich, which was an off-shoot of the Germanen Order founded in 1912 by Theodor Fritsch. Eckart too was influenced by the doctrines of the Thule society.

leader of the party, which he renamed the Nationalsozialistische Deutsche Arbeiterpartei (NSDAP). Hitler had, even before his joining the party, attended Feder's lectures on economic subjects and wrote later in his Mein Kampf (1925/6) of this occasion:

> For the first time in my life I heard a discussion which dealt with the principles of stock-exchange capital and capital which was used for loan activities …The absolute separation of stock-exchange capital from the economic life of the nation would make it possible to oppose the process of internationalization in German business without at the same time attacking capital as such, for to do this would jeopardize the foundations of our national independence. I clearly saw what was developing in Germany and I realized then that the stiffest fight we would have to wage would not be against the enemy nations but against international capital.[3]

In the Foreword to the original 1923 edition of the current work, *Der deutsche Staat*, Hitler wrote that in this work the National Socialist movement had indeed acquired its "catechism".[4]

In 1920, Hitler, along with Feder and Drexler, composed the 25 point '*Programme of the NSDAP*'. This programme rejected the Treaty of Versailles and called for a reunification of German peoples along with an exclusion of aliens, especially Jews, from national life. In February 1920, Hitler held a rally in which he presented the programme to the German people. Later, in 1927, Feder published a comprehensive version of the programme entitled Das Programm der NSDAP und seine weltanschaulichen Grundlagen.[5] In 1923, Feder offered a further elaboration of his national economic views in the present work, *Der deutsche Staat*

---

3 Adolf Hitler, *Mein Kampf*, tr. James Murphy, London: Hurst and Blackett, 1939, pp.168,171.
4 See below p.17.
5 This work was translated by E.T.S. Dugdale as *The Programme Of The Nsdap And Its General Conceptions*, Munich, 1932.

Introduction

auf nationaler und sozialer Grundlage, which was re-issued in 1932 in the "Nationalsozialistische Bibliothek" series[6]

Feder took part in Hitler's failed Beer Hall Putsch against the Bavarian government in 1923 but was only fined 50 marks for unlawful assumption of authority since he had acted, for a day, as the new "finance minister". In 1924, he was elected a representative to the parliament. In parliament, he demanded the confiscation of Jewish property and the freezing of interest-rates. which were key elements of the anti-capitalist programme of the party. In 1926 Hitler entrusted Feder with the editorial direction of a series of books on National Socialist ideology under the title "Nationalsozialistische Bibliothek" (National Socialist Library). In 1931, Feder was appointed chairman of the economic council of the NSDAP. But gradually, under pressure from big industrialists like Gustav Krupp, Fritz Thyssen and Emil Kirdorf, Hitler decided to distance himself from Feder's socialist ideas.[7] With Hitler's strategic alliance with big industrialists and capital, even foreign capital, for his intended war on Bolshevism, Feder lost most of his influence on the party since foreign banks especially would not have supported Feder's plans for a nationalised interest-free banking system. The loss of interest in Feder's economic policies among the party members is evidenced in Hans Reupke's book *Der Nationalsozialismus und die Wirtschaft* (1931), where the author stated that it was no longer necessary to deal with the "breaking of interest slavery" in "the extreme form in which it first emerged".[8]

Thus, when Hitler assumed power in 1933, Feder was not named Economics Minister but rather only State Secretary in the Economics Ministry. However, Feder published in 1933 a collection of his essays entitled *Kampf gegen die Hochfinanz*

---

6 I have for my translation used the 1932 edition, vol.35 of the "Nationalsozialistische Bibliothek" series.
7 For the part played by big industries in Hitler's rise to power see G. Hallgarten, "Adolf Hitler and German heavy industry 1931-1933", *Journal of Economic History*, 12 (1952).
8 H. Reupke, *Der Nationalsozialismus und die Wirtschaft*, Berlin, 1931, pp.29ff.

as well as a book on the Jews called *Die Juden*. In 1934, the influential banker Hjalmar Schact was made Economics Minister since his contacts with the big industrialists made him more useful to Hitler in his rearmament aims than Feder with his stark anti-capitalist doctrines. Feder's subordination to Hjalmar Schacht was indeed a concrete sign of his fall from grace. After the Knight of the Long Knives in 1934, when left-wing nationalists like Gregor Strasser were assassinated, Feder withdrew from the government. In 1936, he was given a new job as professor at the Technical University in Berlin which he maintained until his death in 1941.

Feder's *Deutsche Staat* is indeed one of the most important treatises on National Socialist economics.[9] However, it has a precedent in the Austro-Hungarian Bohemian German, Rudolf Jung's work, *Der Nationale Sozialismus* (1919). Rudolf Jung (1882-1945) was a civil engineer from Jihlava (in the current Czech Republic and former Austro-Hungarian Empire) who joined the Bohemian Deutsche Arbeiter Partei (DAP) in 1909. The DAP was founded in 1903 in Aussig (now Ústí nad Labem in the Czech Republic) by Germans threatened by the increasing Jewish and Czech influence in the empire. It was renamed Deutsche Nationalsozialistische Arbeiter Partei (DNSAP) in 1918. Jung's work *Der Nationale Sozialismus: seine Grundlagen, sein Werdegang und seine Ziele* (1919) was intended as a German nationalist answer to Marx's *Das Kapital*.[10] The work is divided into two parts, the first dealing with 'The Foundations of National Socialism' and the second with 'The Development and Goals of National Socialism'. Jung's nationalism focusses

---

9   The closest to National Socialist economics is the Social Credit movement founded in Britain by C.H. Douglas (1879-1952), whose work *Economic Democracy* was published in 1920 (see F. Hutchison and B. Burkitt, *The Political Economy of Social Credit and Guild Socialism*, London: Routledge, 1997). Douglas influenced Oswald Mosley's British Union of Fascists in the thirties (see Kerry Bolton, "Breaking the bondage of interest, part 2", *Counter-Currents,* August 11, 2011, http://www.counter-currents.com/2011/08/breaking-the-bondage-of-interesta-right-answer-to-usury-part-2/

10   It was on his suggestion that Hitler changed the name of the German branch of the DAP in 1920 to Nationalsozialistische Deutsche Arbeiterpartei (NSDAP).

Introduction

on social and economic questions and, exactly like Feder, Jung stresses the difference between income derived from real work and that arising from interest.[11] His strong socialist and anti-Jewish viewpoint is evident throughout this work:

> All non-socialist parties are based in the main on "individualism", i.e. the demand for the greatest possible freedom and lack of constraint of the individual. Economically it is expressed in Manchester liberalism and, further, in Mammonism. The ruthless ruler who is tormented by no pang of conscience is the goal, the weaker man falls thereby under the wheels. Now, since the Jew is the most ruthless, he can fare best thereby. Thus all non-socialist anti-Jewish orientations unwillingly support the rise of Jewry to world-rulership.[12]

Further, democracy itself is the vehicle of Jewish international capitalism:

> If we were to sum up, we might say that the entire international democracy whose alleged ideals the major press and parties represent and on whose flag they swear, is nothing but the political crystallisation of the Jewish spirit and, in the final analysis, serves no other goal but the establishment of the world-rule of Jewry.[13]

Another writer who contributed to the exact identification of the Jewish constitution of international high finance was Heinrich Pudor (1865-1943), who also wrote under the pseudonym Heinrich Scham (the German translation of the Latin "pudor"). Pudor was a vegetarian and naturist who, from 1912, published several anti-Semitic pamphlets and books including an extensive series on the international connections between the

---

11 Feder's manifesto on interest-slavery was interestingly published in the same year as Jung's work on National Socialism.
12 Rudolf Jung, *Der Nationale Sozialismus*, Munich, 1922, p.187f.
13 *Ibid.*, 53f.

various Jewish high financiers.[14] Feder refers sympathetically to Pudor in the present work.[15] However, Pudor's magazine *Swastika* was banned in 1933 by the National Socialists for its criticisms of the National Socialist leadership and the regime's surprising toleration of Jews. Further, five issues of the series on Jewish high finance were banned including no.13, *Neues über Br. Roosevelt und seine jüdischen und Kommunistischen Verbindungen*, and no.49, *Judendämmerung. "Juden unerwünscht". Keine jüdischen Rechtsanwälte mehr. Ende der Judenfinanz in Deutschland*, on account of what a state official, Raymund Schmidt, described as Pudor's "no longer opportune polemical methods which were indeed exploited by the English recently for the purpose of counter-propaganda.[16]

Feder's treatise on national economy, like Rudolf Jung's, is remarkable for its strong moral foundation and its formulation of National Socialism as a movement for social justice as well as for national regeneration. Unlike capitalism with its "soul-destroying materialistic spirit of egoism and avarice with all its concomitant corrupting manifestations in all fields of our public,

---

14 The pamphlets that he self-published (in Leipzig) in this series, "Die internationalen verwandtschaftlichen Beziehungen der jüdischen Hochfinanz" (The international kindred relationships of Jewish high finance'), between 1933 and 1940 present short historical accounts of the different branches of Jewry in various countries of Europe as well as in America. For instance, the first pamphlet is on *Das Haus Rothschild*, numbers two to four on *Ginsberg und Günsberg und Asher Ginzberg*, five to eight on *Jakob Schiff und die Warburgs und das New Yorker Bankhaus Kuhn, Loeb & Co.*, nine to ten on *Amsterdamer und Oppenheimer Juden*, eleven on *Französische Finanzjuden*, twelve on *Tschechoslowakische Finanzjuden*, fourteen on *Rumänische Finanzjuden, fifteen on Lessing und Moses Mendelsohn und das Bankhaus Mendelssohn & Co.*, seventeen on Polnische Finanzjuden, eighteen on *Schwedische Finanzjuden, nineteen on Holländische und belgische Finanzjuden*, twenty on *Frankfurter Finanzjuden und die I.G. Farben*, twenty-one to twenty-three on *Englische Finanzjuden*, thirty-four to thirty-eight and forty-three to forty-four on *Tshechische Finanzjuden* and thirty-nine to forty-two on *Ungarische Finanzjuden*. In addition, he published, in Halle, a similar work on *Amerikanische Finanzjuden* (1936).
15 See below p.120.
16 "nicht mehr zeitgemäßen Kampfmethoden, die sogar von den Engländern in jüngster Zeit zum Zwecke der Gegenpropaganda ausgeschlachtet wurden" (see Gerd Simon, "Chronologie, Pudor, Heinrich", http://homepages.uni-tuebingen.de/gerd.simon/ChrPudor.pdf, p.19f.)

economic and cultural life"[17] and unlike Marxism, which insists that everything should belong to the One, which might be either the State or Mammon controlling it, National Socialism wishes to revert to the mediaeval and Prussian dictum of *suum cuique*, 'to each his own', whereby each person will earn as much as he deserves according to his performance of work, with the fullest possible responsibility, as a duty. Economically, this moral doctrine is translated into the doctrine of serving "the public interest" before self-interest. Not profitability but fulfilment of demand is the National Socialistic basis of the economy.

Unlike Marxism, National Socialism will not prohibit private property but respect it as the privilege of the creative and productive Aryan man. On the other hand, the mobile Jewish mind has no deep connection with the land but rather exploits the productions and property of the natives financially through all sorts of legal claims, bonds and mortgages, whereby "property" is turned into a profitable "possession". In order to counter these avaricious strategies of the Jews, the National Socialist state will enforce limitations on the right to property, personal or commercial, so that in all cases the welfare of the whole, the nation, rather than of individuals will be first served. In Feder's discussion of the party's programme in Part II, we note that, since the social policy is "the welfare of the whole", the financial policy of the National Socialist state is accordingly directed against those financial powers who tend to develop "a state within the state". As he puts it:

> In the last and deepest analysis, it is a matter of the battle of two world-views that are expressed through two fundamentally different intellectual structures – the productive and creative spirit and the mobile avaricious spirit. The creative spirit rooted in the soil and yet again overcoming the world in metaphysical experience finds its principal representatives in Aryan man – the avaricious,

---

17 All page-references are to the present edition.

rootless commercial and materialistic spirit directed purely to the this-worldly finds its principal representative in the Jew.

The strength of Germany before the war was due to its unity under Bismarck and its efficient industrial sector. This advantage was undermined by the dependence of the economy on the credit system of the banks and "the inventors and bearers of the modern credit system" are the Jews. The mediaeval system of credit was based on the belief ("credo") of the creditor that his money could be used to greater economic advantage by the debtor whereby the debtor, if successful in his enterprise, may return a share of his profits in gratitude to the creditor. Standardised interest, on the other hand, was forbidden by the Church as usury. Feder advocates a return to the conception of money as a token of "performed work" or of a product so that money cannot, independently of any work, be hoarded for the purpose of being lent out later at interest.

Feder further points out that it is the stock-market that lies at the basis of the alienation of capital from work:

> Anonymisation – the depersonalisation of our economy through the stock-marketable form of the public limited company – has to a certain degree separated capital from work, the share-holder knows in the rarest instances something of his factory, he has only the one-sided interest in the profitability of his money when he has invested it in the form of shares.

Apart from the indifference of the shareholder to the quality of the goods produced by the company in which he invests, the market in general has diverted production from its legitimate task of fulfilling real needs to that of stirring up - through the Jewish market-crier's technique of advertising - artificial needs among the public that will bring in greater profits. This fundamental transformation of national economics has been supported in

Introduction

academic circles by Jewish scholars who restrict their economic analyses to descriptions of the current economic system rather than investigating its social and political legitimacy. This sort of intellectual subversion is further continued by the Jewish intelligentsia in the fields of art, entertainment and the press.

The major source of the current distress of Germany is indeed the interest owed to large loan capital. The burden of interest has indebted entire nations to international high finance and forced them to become interest-collectors for the latter which they do by taxing the working people ever harder. Feder rightly calls this false economic process an "international fraud". The power of international finance has however grown so great that it was able to encircle Germany as soon as it perceived that its currency was rising in strength and independence. Once they succeeded in militarily defeating Germany, the international financial powers then enforced further enormous debt burdens on it through the Treaty of Versailles. Feder therefore proposes the cancellation of the payment of the interest on these debts to the Allies. Indeed, the remedy to the interest burdens of all nations to international finance is the legal abolition of interest. And this is simultaneously the solution to the Jewish question itself:

> The solution of the interest problem is the solution of the Jewish question. The solution of the interest problem in the sense of our explanations is the breaking of the Jewish world-rule, because it smashes the power of world Jewry – its financial power.

The fullest representation of the socio-economic interests of a nation should be the state, and its industries should be models of efficiency and commercial success. One example of such an industry in Germany is indeed the transport industry and especially the German railways. Unlike Bolshevism, which seeks to control all production, the National Socialist state will, through the establishment of storage and distribution cooperatives under state supervision, remove only the avaricious interference of private commerce between production and consumption. As the means of exchange necessary for the exchange of goods, money will be under the control of the state through a nationalised state bank.

Instead of borrowing money from private banks, the state should, in the case of all large public works projects, finance the latter though the issuance of interest-free notes of its own. The Reichsbank's sovereignty of issuing notes must be regained through nationalisation. Freed of interest-burdens to banks, the state will ultimately be able to operate in a mostly tax-free manner. Taxes will be restricted to the coverage of non-productive tasks such as the administration of justice, the police system, medical and educational systems, if the commercial enterprises of the state such as the railways post and telegraph, mining and forestry do not present surpluses wherewith to pay for these tasks. International transactions should be conducted through a clearing system rather like that of the international postal union "without the international finance benefiting two or three times in all these simple mercantile operations and becoming big and fat at the cost of the productive nations".

But the state must be powerful if it is to effect any reforms. Unfortunately, the Weimar Republic has abjectly accepted the monstrous burden of guilt after the war with the result that "the members of the Chosen People can, on these reparations, forever lead a glamorous work-free life in all the countries of the world at the cost of German work.". The crisis faced by Germany after the war was facilitated by parliamentarianism and Mammonism. The "great democratic lie of the capacity of the people for self-government" is to be combated along with the real capitalistic rulers of democracies. Marxism likewise is a sham socialist system that employs the dissatisfaction of those exploited by Mammonism for the benefit of the "handlers for international capital" in order to "divert from themselves the hatred of the exploited".

Introduction

The majority of the principal Marxists as well as Mammonists are Jews, and so "The Jewish question is becoming a world-question on whose solution the welfare and woe of the nations will be dependent". The solution of this question cannot be through violence since "indeed one cannot kill the plague bacillus individually, one can only eradicate it by cutting off its life necessities from it". A suggestion of what might be done to reduce their ill-earned gains is contained in point 17 of the party's programme which envisages creation of legal possibilities of confiscating if necessary land that was acquired in an illegal way or not administered according to the viewpoint of the welfare of the people. This is directed thus mainly against the Jewish land speculation companies.

Further, a removal of Jews from all public positions will cause no difficulty to the nation since "the real vitally important productive activity in industry and agriculture, in the professions and administration, is almost entirely free of Jews". Concomitant with the removal of Jews from the "national body" is the enforcement of new citizenship laws whereby the citizenship rights will be "acquired" by the citizens and not merely granted to them. Thus only those who pledge themselves to the German community and culture and do not continue an adherence to another nation can obtain these rights.

The National Socialist state will be a strong state that includes all the German tribes and its power will be concentrated in a strong leader, or autocrat, who embodies "the highest responsibility"[18] since the German people have traditionally wanted a strong leader, and monarchs are not always to be relied upon. The leader of the National Socialist state, on the other hand, is not envisaged as a permanent ruler but one chosen only for the re-establishment of order and prosperity of a debilitated nation. After he has accomplished his goals he may step aside to let

---

18 The "Führer principle" was championed also by Rudolf Jung in his Nationale Sozialismus, p.177f.

other rulers take his place under the constitution. Indeed, the National Socialist state may be characterised as a constitutional autocracy. The constitutional aspect of the state will be used especially to ensure an effective labour law and social insurance. Obviously, in a German national state, no members of foreign races can assume the leadership of state affairs.

Feder is aware of the adverse reaction of the international financiers to such autarkic measures but he believes that a transformation of interest-bearing bonds into interest-free bank assets or postal cheque accounts wherewith foreign creditors can be paid will avert the wrath of the latter. He also suggests that boycotts can be overcome through transactions with neutral countries. As for military action, he believes that it is not likely to be pursued by the foreign creditor nations since if the German people saw the French or Jewish tax collector sitting in every tax- and pension office, and if the best cows were taken from the stalls of the farmers by these foreign oppressors – then the anger and indignation would perhaps become soon so strong that one night would sweep the foreign spectre away with a bloody broom and free Germany.

We see that, in spite of the lucidity of his economic doctrines, Feder rather underestimated the unforgiving nature of the Mammon that he was striving against. In keeping with Feder's doctrines, the Nationalist Socialist state officially cancelled the war debt to the Allied nations and sought, from 1933 on, to combat the cumulative deflation by the creation of money and work.[19] Work was created by increasing public works activity, such as notably the building of super- highways, and other construction and agricultural projects. These projects were financed, as Feder had recommended, by the issuance of government bills.[20] The production of armaments especially was

---

19   See G. Senft, "Anti-Kapitalismus von Rechts? - Eine Abrechnung mit Gottfried Feders 'Brechung der Zinsknechtschaft'", *Zeitschrift für Sozialökonomie*, 106 (1995), pp.18-32.
20   According to Henry Liu: "through an independent monetary policy of sovereign credit

Introduction

spurred by the use of the so-called 'Mefo' bills - named after Schacht's Metallurgische Forschungsgesellschaft (Mefo), which served as a government holding company.[21] These bills were used by government contractors for payment of their needs and were valid as a form of currency. As a result of these economic strategies, as Overy notes, "the banks increasingly became mere intermediaries, holding government stock and helping in the job of keeping bills circulating in the way that the government wanted."[22] Tax levels were simultaneously reduced for farmers, small businesses and heavy industry through the "remission of taxes already paid".[23] However, Hitler was also dependent in his ambitious rearmament plans on foreign finance, which certainly would not have accepted Feder's insistence on an abolition of interest.[24]

The National Socialist economy was an increasingly state-controlled one that sought to avoid inflation by controlling prices and wages and foreign trade. Autarkic restrictions on imports were offset by bilateral barter agreements. Whether the war that began two years after the 1937 edition of Feder's work was, as Feder's view of the role of international finance in the first World War would suggest, another effort to punish Germany's financial independence under National Socialism or whether it was indeed secretly willed by the international financiers

---

and a full-employment public-works program, the Third Reich was able to turn a bankrupt Germany, stripped of overseas colonies it could exploit, into the strongest economy in Europe within four years, even before armament spending began" (Henry C.K. Liu, "Nazism and the German economic miracle," *Asia Times Online*, 24 May 2005, http://www.atimes.com/atimes/Global_Economy/GE24Dj01.html).

21 Hitler's eagerness to rearm Germany is not surprising in the light of the eastern expansionist and anti-Bolshevist foreign political aims outlined by him already in *Mein Kampf*, Vol.II, Ch.14.
22 R.J. Overy, *The Nazi Economic Recovery 1932-1938*, Cambridge: Cambridge University Press, 1996, p.43.
23 *Ibid.*, p.38.
24 See the web-log by "Scanners", "Gottfried Feder und das zinslose Geld", http://www.utopia.de/blog/umweltpolitik/gottfried-feder-und-das-zinslose. The western financial powers may have partly supported Hitler's effort to check the westward spread of Bolshevism. For American involvement in National Socialist finance, for example, see Anthony C. Sutton, *Wall Street and the rise of Hitler*, Sudbury: Bloomfield Books, 1976.

for their own geopolitical ends, the increasing losses suffered by Germany in the course of it certainly provoked Hitler into attempting to "sweep the foreign spectre away with a bloody broom", as Feder had predicted.

But neither Feder nor Hitler may have foreseen the severity of the revenge - more cruel since more lasting than that after the first World War - that the international Jewish interests would take on Germany after its defeat in 1945. While Feder hoped that other nations of the world will also eventually follow the German example and "mankind, freed of the Jewish oppression, will experience an age of unprecedented prosperity – and, above all, Germany - the heart of the world", the opposite of that indeed has occurred, since most of Europe has been turned into "a slave, fellaheen, bondman and servant of the all-Jewish world-power" (p.62). And the heart of Germany itself, drained by a tyrannical psychological control of its population, has virtually stopped beating.

Alexander Jacob

The Rise of the N.S.D.A.P.

Adolf Hitler was born on April 20th, 1889, at Braunau on the Inn, a village of the old Bavaria. His father was the orphaned child of a poor peasant and worked his way up to being a Customs Official. His mother came from a German peasant family. When he was 13 years old he lost his father, and four years later his mother. Adolf Hitler was then a scholar at the Realschule at Linz on the Danube, after leaving the National School. It had been his father's wish that he should become an official, but his own desire was to be an artist. His mother's death obliged him without further delay to earn his own living.

At 17 years old Hitler went to Vienna, where he aimed to become an architect. He earned a living by his own efforts, first as a builder's labourer, mixing the mortar, then as an architect's draughtsman. At 18 years old he was already taking an interest in politics; he became anti-Marxist, but so far took no leading part. From his earliest youth Hitler had been passionately Nationalist, and his hope was to combine the social experiences of his working period with his nationalist convictions. For several years he lived in Vienna in extreme poverty.

In 1912 he migrated to Munich, where he was a student. He had never known youthful enjoyments, but ever since the day when he left home with 50 kronen in his pocket, labour and privation had been his lot.

In February, 1914, he succeeded in getting free from the obligation to serve in the Austrian Army. Six months later war broke out. He immediately volunteered for service in the German Army, and obtained, by a direct appeal to King Ludwig of Bavaria, permission to enter a Bavarian regiment as a volunteer for the war. On October 10th, 1914, the new regiment marched forth.

On December 2nd, 1914, the 25-years old volunteer was awarded the Iron Cross, 2nd Class. In recognition of his bravery in the attack on the 'Bayernwald' and in the other engagements near Wytschaete, he was ordered to take on duty as a despatch-carrier, which demanded special courage and reliability, for reports had often to be carried across open ground under heavy fire. This quickly made his name known throughout the regiment beyond the narrow circle of his comrades.

On October 7th, 1916, he was wounded by a shell splinter. In March, 1917, he returned to his regiment. He received several other distinctions, including a *Regiments-Diplom* for special bravery in the fights near Fontaines, and finally the Iron Cross, Class I.

On October 14th, 1918 he was severely injured along with many comrades in his regiment by Mustard Gas which the British were then using for the first time, and he was temporarily blinded. Whilst he was in hospital the Revolution broke out.

On this Hitler resolved to become a politician. In 1919 he joined with a small party consisting of 6 men and on it he founded the National Socialist German Workers' Party. He drew up in outline the Programme of the new movement, and settled its character and aims.

The Nucleus: Seven Men

In September, 1919, Adolf Hitler made his first speech to seven men; he then addressed audiences of 11, 25, 47; in December 111; in January, 1920, 270, and shortly afterwards 400.

On 14th November, 1920, he spoke at a mass-meeting of 1700. He now organised the propaganda of the young Party, which after a year's work numbered 64 members. A year later — 1920 — it had already reached 3000 members.

Hitler's propagandist activity in Munich was such that he was finally addressing mass-meetings three times a week, and on Mondays he carried on a course of instruction. He attacked first and foremost the folly of Versailles, and denied the assertions of the Marxists, the Centre Party, etc. that it was possible to fulfil that Treaty. He pilloried the slogan of these Parties — "Give up your arms, and the others will also disarm". He spoke on the assumption that after arms had been given up by us the rest would continue to arm, — if not with their own money, then with the millions wrung from the completely disarmed German nation. Whilst opposing the propaganda of the S.P.D. and Centre in favour of signing the Treaty, he prophecied that the Ruhr would be occupied, whatever we signed.

1921

This year was marked by the foundation of the first local groups at Rosenheim and Landshut. Hitler organised the first body of men to protect the Party, and began his fight against the Separatist movement in Bavaria. Our leader also addressed a meeting of over 5000 in the Circus in Munich.

He declared at his meetings that fulfilment of the Treaty would not help, as the S.P.D., Centre and Volkspartei asserted, to build up German prosperity in peace and quiet, but that the result of that foolish policy was bound to be inflation on a large scale, involving immense injury to German industry. Hitler's assertion that the black-red Government was planning to de-nationalise the State Railways was declared to be a 'bare-faced lie'. An attempt at a revolt within the Party was defeated. Hitler drafted the new Constitution of the Party, which gave him dictatorial powers.

Social Democracy, which was unable to continue to ignore the name of Hitler, now attempted to get rid of its bug-bear by methods of terrorism. There were sanguinary collisions at the meetings, in which our leader's iron nerves maintained the upper hand. An invincible body-guard was formed in the course of them, which thenceforward was named the 'Storm Detachment'.

1922

Whilst the conquest of Munich was proceeding, the movement was beginning to spread throughout the rest of Bavaria. Hitler rejected all overtures, by way of compromise, to join up with other Parties. He gradually destroyed all similar 'nationalist' party formations, and made the National Socialist movement supreme over them.

In October, 1922, Hitler marched at the head of 800 men to Coburg, and twice in 24 hours utterly crushed the Red Terror in that town.

Adolf Hitler declared then publicly that we were rushing headlong in the direction of inflation, which he had foreseen as the result of the policy of the black-red coalition. He became known as the most dangerous and best hated enemy of the system. Social Democracy and the Centre Party ceased defending themselves by argument, and adopted a policy of defamation.

1923

In January, 1923, the first great Party Conference was held, and the first banners of the Party were consecrated. The Storm Detachment was formally incorporated.

The Party propaganda was exhaustively studied and improved, and the permanent principles of the organisation were settled and established. Adherents gathered round Hitler in large numbers, the majority of whom are today his stedfast partners in the struggle. The attacks on him were meanwhile pursued with increasing determination; he found himself in prison for the first time on the charge of disturbing the meetings of his adversaries; he was constantly fined. Nevertheless he never for one moment ceased fighting against the system.

During the summer of 1923 Adolf Hitler proceeded to break down the Red Terror in the majority of the towns in Bavaria; Ratisbon, Hof, Bayreuth, Nurenberg, Furth, Ingolstadt,

The Rise of the N.S.D.A.P.

Wurzburg, Schweinfurt, — often at the cost of bloodshed in street fights, in which he defeated the Social-democratic and Communist terrorist bands.

His struggle against the incompetent Government of the Reich was accompanied by bitter accusations. He prophecied the ill-success of the Government's feeble resistance in the matter of the Ruhr, and constantly attacked the stupid policy of an understanding with France, and that of fulfilment. He never failed to point out the necessity of an understanding with England and Italy.

In November, 1923, Adolf Hitler made his attempt to overthrow the system. The rising failed, and Hitler was arrested.

1924

The great Trial took place in Munich in March, 1924. Though found guilty on the facts, our leader achieved overwhelming moral justification. Hitler's defence influenced the Court to such an extent, and his assumption of sole and exclusive responsibility was so convincing, that the speech of the counsel indicting him turned into a remarkable testimony to his honourable motives. The Judge however condemned hirn to a period of detention.

The National Socialist Party suffered by the loss of its leader. Its adversaries were convinced that the movement was done for, and took courage to sign the infamous Dawes Pact, thus deliberately starting the system of the plundering of Germany which was brought to a head in the Young Plan. What a triumph for the Social Democrats and the Centre! The objective of the enslavement of Germany was apparently achieved!

In vain Hitler tried through his associates, who were at liberty, to put up a fight against the Dawes Pact. In vain he made them declare in public that the assurances of the Centre Party, the S.P.D. and the Volkspartei, that the foreign loans under the Plan would increase national prosperity, that unemployment would cease, that wages would be raised and taxes reduced, that agriculture would be saved, were merely a deception of the nation. In vain he made them point out that the Dawes Pact was bound to increase poverty, since the interest on the loans would cripple industry, whilst the loans themselves merely served the purpose of fulfilling the financial obligations under the Plan; bankruptcy and unemployment would increase, wages would sink, prices and taxation would rise still further, and the farmers would be faced with utter ruin and be forced to part with all they possessed.

1925

By February 27th, 1925, Adolf Hitler's call for the re-birth of the Party went forth, and he made his first speech after his imprisonment before an audience of 4000 persons.

The National Socialist movement had been broken up after the events of November 9th, and all its property and money had been confiscated; so that Adolf Hitler now started with nothing in hand to rebuild the Party from its foundations. Vorwärts and Germania in Berlin made fun of his efforts and mocked at the "fool whom imprisonment had made mad". Nevertheless the reconstruction of the Party proceeded with great rapidity under Hitler's leadership. The old leaders gathered faithfully round him once more. Hitler stimulated the Party press into fresh activity.

By December, 1925, the Party numbered 27,000 members. The Centre and the Social Democrats in alarm decreed that the leader should not speak in public for two years.

1926

June of this year saw the first Conference of the Party since Hitler's imprisonment. The bourgeois world were still convinced that the policy of fulfilment would save Germany and that the Dawes Pact would revive industry. The Marxists were convinced that their domination was unshakable.

The Rise of the N.S.D.A.P.

President von Hindenburg separated from his supporters and marched off with the Centre and S.P.D. The Party carried on the struggle; by the end of the year it numbered 49,000 members.

1927

The order forbidding Hitler to speak in public was withdrawn, since it was found impossible to enforce it. He addressed numbers of mass meetings. Each month saw the Party more and more firmly consolidated. Developments all round proved with greater and greater force that Hitler had been right. The Dawes Pact was unmasked, and its consequences were terrific. The Social Democrats and Centre Party attempted to save what might be saved by means of lies and abuse.

In August Hitler summoned a Party Conference at Nurenberg, which proved a great success. By the end of the year the Party numbered 72,000 members.

1928

Adolf Hitler led his Party in an intensified assault on the existing system. National Socialism was now the inexorable enemy of the destroyers of Germany within and without. Hitler directed his attack especially against the senseless ruining of the farmers and middle classes. He prophecied the catastrophe which would fall upon the home markets. He declared at hundreds of meetings again and again that the policy of fulfilment was lunacy, and that its consequences would mean death and ruin to German industry. The Social Democrats and Centre mocked and jeered in their attempt to get their revenge. Their lies and abuse were directed at Hitler personally.

By the end of the year the membership numbered 108,000, and 12 members of the Party sat in the Reichstag.

1929

Adolf Hitler continued his fight with the existing system with untiring energy. The Press of the Party was perfected, the Storm

Detachment increased, the SS formations strengthened, and the propaganda intensified. The doctrines of National Socialism began to penetrate deeply into the national consciousness.

On August 4th the second Party Conference took place at Nurenberg on a tremendous scale. Hitler attacked the black-red system with ever increasing energy and stood forth without a rival as the most powerful leader against all that was meant by 'Democracy'. All attempts to oust him from the leadership of the Party were crushed.

By the end of the year the Party numbered 178,000 members.

1930

The struggle against the Young Plan was in full swing. Hindenburg defended it with energy, asserting that by it Germany would be saved, that German industry would revive, that unemployment would be stemmed, that the farmers would breathe again, and that it would be possible to lighten taxation.

Adolf Hitler described such views as unreal and fatal; he prophecied the contrary. His Party proceeded to enlighten the nation amidst severe fighting. The opponents replied with a stream of lies.

The Elections to the Reichstag took place on September 14th, 1930. The Party polled 6½ million votes, and 107 members were elected. Its internal organisation was stronger than ever. A few minor attempts at revolt, promoted from outside, were promptly crushed by Hitler, and those who would not submit unconditionally were expelled.

The Centre Party, which had now delivered itself into the hands of the S.P.D. for good or ill, began to excite the Church against Hitler. Bishops and Priests, belonging to the Centre Party, started a fanatical attack against the National Socialist movement, excommunicated its adherents, and even refused them Christian burial. Hitler held unshakably to his conviction that the Centre spelt ruin for Germany, and continued his fight against it with even greater determination than before. He sternly rejected any attempt to extort some modification of his opinions from him.

By the end of the year the Party numbered 389,000 members.

1931

The fight against the Young Plan continued. The consequences foreseen by Hitler became a reality.

The Government began to administrate by means of emergency measures, thinking thus to save industry. Sharp disputes followed, in which Adolf Hitler again pointed out the fatal consequences of that policy. In a few months — a few weeks even — he was proved right.

Meanwhile numbers of National Socialist newspapers had started into life, and the central publishing office of the Party had gradually grown to be a vast enterprise. The organisation had become highly efficient, and the Storm Detachment had in course of time reached a high stage of development. Our opponents wallowed in lies, and were allowing orders for goods to be placed in France.

By the end of the year 1931 the membership of the Hitler Party reached 806,000, a month later to 862,000, and again a month later to 920,000. On the day of the Election there were something like a million members, and untold millions of supporters at the polls.

The man who was once a poor worker and later a soldier at the front has thus in barely twelve years built up the greatest political organisation which Germany has ever seen. The sole resources against this man which his opponents can employ are lies and defamation. And he has always won so far in spite of all the lies, and this time he has come near to being elected President of the Reich.

Has anyone in the whole history of Germany ever accomplished a similar achievement in twelve years, in face of opposition from Party, high finance, Capital, Press, public opinion, bureaucracy, lies, terrorism, and persecution?

This was no sheltered child; from his earliest years he has been a man in the highest sense of the word, relying solely on his own strength.

Preface

At Weimar in 1926 the Council of the Party decided to publish a series of pamphlets, dealing in a concise form with the fundamental questions affecting every aspect of political life in Germany. Our intention was, and is, to present a consistent and complete picture of the attitude of National Socialism towards the various tasks of our public life, and of the means by which it hopes to remove its errors and defects.

Our task is therefore to examine exhaustively how it stands, then to enquire scientifically whence it originated, and finally, with creative inspiration, to answer the fateful question, what then? The high aim of these pamphlets is to indicate new methods for the life of the State, for finance and economics; to set on high a 'rocher de bronze' in the midst of the chaos, to form a stock of clear knowledge by close study, so that out of it all may emerge a united political will.

At the great Meeting on August 31st, 1927, Adolf Hitler declared emphatically : "Questions of Programme do not affect the Council of Administration; the Programme is fixed, and I shall never suffer changes in the principles of the movement, as laid down in its Programme." With this decisive pronouncement on the part of our Leader I associate myself whole-heartedly, for nothing is more dangerous to the life and striking force of a movement such as ours, than that, as time goes on, its fixed Programme should be subjected to negative criticism.

No man who feels that he cannot go the whole way with us in the Jewish question, in our fight against high finance, the Dawes Pact and the pauperising policy, or in any other questions contained in our Programme, or is inclined to barter the liberty of the German nation through the League of Nations, the Locarno

Pact, by compromise and cowardice, need apply to us; his place is outside the N.S.D.A.P. We utterly reject the 'superior private knowledge' which such as he are so ready to air in platform oratory and journalistic out-pourings.

A man who agrees fundamentally with our principles may perhaps have scruples about a few minor details, for we cannot expect everyone to agree absolutely on all questions, especially in an aggressive political movement.

It is, however, a different matter when political enemies make mincemeat of some one point by odious misrepresentation quite beside the point, as has indeed happened. In such a case an official commentary is necessary.

We refuse to vary our Programme for reasons of expediency, as other Parties do, to suit so-called altered conditions. We intend to make conditions suit our Programme, by mastering them.

I have been commissioned by Adolf Hitler to issue this series of pamphlets, which are to form the official literature of the Party.

I have included the official Manifesto of the Party of March 6th, 1930; also my reply to ten questions set us by the Deutsche Tageszeitung, the leading organ of the Reichslandbund. That newspaper accepted my replies.

This is the best and most effective way to dispose of all the lies about our ill-disposition towards ownership and inheritance of landed property in Germany.

The Official Party Manifesto

On the Position of the N.S.DAP. with Regard to the Farming Population and Agriculture

1. The Importance of the Farming Class and Agriculture for Germany.

The German nation derive a considerable portion of their food from importation of foreign food-stuffs. Before the world War we managed to pay for these imports with our industrial exports, our trade, and our deposits of capital abroad. The outcome of the war put an end to this possibility.

Today we are paying for our imported food mostly with the help of foreign loans, which drive the German nation deeper and deeper in debt to the international financiers who provide credits. If things go on as they are, the German people will become more and more impoverished.

The only possibility of escaping from this thraldom lies in the ability of Germany to produce essential food stuffs at home. Increased production by German agriculture is therefore a question of life and death for the German nation. Moreover a country population, economically sound and highly productive, is essential for our industry, which will in future have more and more to look for openings in the home market.

We also regard the country population as the bearer of the inheritance of health, the source of the nation's youth, and as the back-bone of its armed strength.

Maintenance of an efficient agricultural class, increasing in numbers as the general population increases, is an essential plank in the National Socialist platform, because our movement considers the welfare of all our people in the generations to come.

2. The Present-Day State's Neglect of the Farming Class and of Agriculture.

Agricultural production, which in itself is capable of being augmented, is being handicapped, because the increasing indebtedness of the farmers prevents their purchasing the necessities of cultivation, and because the fact that farming does not pay removes the inducement to increase production.

The reasons why farming fails to give a sufficient return for the labour are to be sought:

1. in the existing fiscal policy, which lays undue burdens on agriculture. This is due to Party considerations, and because the Jewish world money market — which really controls parliamentary democracy in Germany — wishes to destroy German agriculture, since this would place the German nation, and especially the working class, at its mercy;

2. in the competition of foreign agriculturists, who work under more favourable conditions, and who are not held in check by a policy of protection for German agriculture;

3. in the extravagant profits made by the large wholesale middlemen, who thrust themselves in between producer and consumer.

4. in the oppressive rates the farmer has to pay for electric power and artificial manures to concerns mainly run by Jews.

The high taxation cannot be met out of the poor return for labour on the land. The farmer is forced to run into debt and to pay usurious interest for loans. He sinks deeper and deeper under this tyranny, and in the end forfeits all that he possesses to the Jew money-lender. The German farming class is being expropriated.

3. In the Reich, the Rights of Land Shall Be Respected and There Shall Be an Agricultural Policy for Germany.

There can be no hope of any sweeping improvement in the conditions of poverty of the country population, or of a revival of agriculture, as long as the German Government is in fact controlled by the international money-magnates, helped by the parliamentary-democratic system of government; for these desire to destroy Germany's strength, which is based on the land.

In the new and very different German State, to which we aspire, the farmers and agriculture will receive the consideration which is due to them owing to the fact that they are a main support of a truly national German State. From this emerge the following requirements:

1. The land of Germany, acquired and defended by the German nation, must be at the service of the German nation, as a home and as a means of livelihood. Those who occupy the land must administer it in this sense.

2. Only members of the German nation may possess land.

3. Land legally acquired by them shall be regarded as inheritable property. To the right to hold property, however, is attached the obligation to use it in the national interest. Special Courts shall be appointed to oversee this obligation; these shall consist of representatives from, all departments of the land-holding class, and one representative of the State.

4. German land may not become an object of financial speculation, nor may it provide an unearned income for its owner. It may only be acquired by him who is prepared to cultivate it himself.

Therefore the State has a right of preemption on every sale of land.

It is forbidden to pledge land to private lenders. The necessary loans for cultivation on easy terms will be granted to farmers either by associations recognised by the State, or by the State itself.

5. Dues will be paid to the State for the use of land according to the extent and quality of the property. This tax on land will obviate any further taxation of landed property.

6. No hard and fast rule can be laid down as to the amount of cultivation. From the point of view of our population policy we require large numbers of small and middle-sized farms. Farming on a large scale, however, has a very essential part to play, and, if it preserves a healthy relation towards the smaller businesses, it is justifiable.

7. A law of inheritance will be required to prevent sub-division of property and an accumulation of debt upon it.

8. The State shall have the right of appropriating land, suitable compensation being granted:

    (a) when not owned by a member of the nation;

    (b) when — by a judgment of the Land Courts — it is held that its owner, by bad farming, is not acting in the national interest;

    (c) for the purpose of settling independent farmers on it, when the owner is not cultivating it himself;

    (d) when it is required for special State purposes in the national interest (e. g., communications, national defence).

Land acquired illegally (according to German law) may be confiscated without compensation.

9. It is the duty of the State to colonise land which has become available, by a scheme based on high considerations of a policy of population. The land shall be allotted to settlers as a hereditary possession under conditions which shall make a livelihood possible. Settlers shall be selected by examination as to their civic and professional suitability. Special favour shall be shown to sons of farmers who have not the right to inherit (see §7).

Colonisation of the eastern frontiers is of extreme importance. In this case the mere establishment of farms will not be sufficient, but it will be necessary to set up market towns in connection with the new branch of industry. This is the only way to provide an opening for making the smaller farms a paying proposition.

It will be the duty of Germany's foreign policy to provide large spaces for the nourishment and settlement of the growing population of Germany.

4. The Farming Class Must Be Raised Economically and Educationally

1. The present poverty of the land population must be at once relieved by remissions of taxation and other emergency measures. Further indebtedness must be stemmed by reducing the rate of interest on loans to that of the pre-war period by law, and by summary action against extortion.

2. It must be the State's policy to see to it that farming be made to pay. German agriculture must be protected by tariffs, State regulation of imports, and a scheme of national training.

The settlement of prices for agricultural produce must be freed from market speculation, and a stop must be put to exploitation of the agricultural interest by the large middlemen, the transfer of whose business to agricultural associations must be encouraged by the State.

It shall be the task of such professional organisations to reduce the running expenses of farmers and increase production. (Provision of implements, manures, seed, breeding stock on favourable conditions, improvements, war against vermin, free advice, chemical research, etc.) The State shall provide full assistance to the organisations in carrying out their task. In particular the State must insist on a considerable reduction in the cost to farmers of artificial manures and electric power.

3. The organisations must also establish the class of farm labourers as members of the farming community by contracts which are just in the social sense. Supervision and arbitration in these matters will be the function of the State. It must be made possible for good labourers to rise to the status of farm-owners. The much called-for improvement in living conditions and wages of farm labourers will ensue as soon as the general farming situation improves. When these conditions take a turn for the better, it will be no longer necessary to employ foreign labour on the land, and this custom will in future be forbidden.

4. The national importance of the farming class requires that the State shall promote technical education in agriculture. (Juvenile institutions, high schools for agriculture, with very favourable terms for youths with talent but no means.)

5. Professional organisations cannot provide all the assistance required by the farming class; only the political movement of the N.S.D.A.P. for German liberty can do this.

The country population are poor because the whole German nation is poor. It is an error to imagine that one single class of workers can escape sharing the fortunes of the German community as a whole, — and a crime to make jealousies between town folk and country folk, who are bound together for good or ill.

Economic assistance under the present political system cannot produce a permanent improvement, for political slavery is at the root our people's poverty, and political methods alone can remove that.

The old political Parties, which were, and are, responsible for the national enslavement, cannot be the leaders on the road to freedom.

There are important economic tasks awaiting professional organisations in our future State; even now they can do much preparatory work in that direction; but for the political struggle of liberation, which is to lay the foundation of a new economic order, they are not suitable; for that struggle will have to be fought out from the point of view not of a single profession, but from that of the whole nation.

The movement which will carry through the political struggle for liberation to the end is the N.S.D.A.P.

Adolf Hitler.

Munich, March 6, 1930.

1. The Policy of the N.S.D.A.P.

On Ownership of Landed Property
A Reply by Gottfried Feder.

The Deutsche Tageszeitung (No. 47) of January 25th, 1930, published a number of questions put to us by the leaders of the Brandenburg Landbund. Their main object was to obtain a definition of the attitude of the N.S.D.A.P. towards private ownership of land, inheritance, raising of credits, tariffs, price regulation, profit-sharing, and towards questions of general social-political and election-tactical interest.

I

In order to allay anxiety with regard to any later arbitrary interpretation of Point 17 of the Party Programme (see p. 19), the first question was put in the following words:

"Is the N.S.D.A.P. prepared to give a guarantee that it will not set its face against ownership of land."

Answer. National Socialism recognises private ownership as a principle, and places it under State protection. It will seek to maintain a healthy combination of all businesses, small and great, in the economic life of the nation.

The spirit of the whole Programme proves clearly that National Socialism, being a convinced and consistent opponent of Marxism, utterly rejects its ruinous central doctrine of general confiscation, and considers a permanent agricultural class to be the best and surest foundation for the national State. But being also a determined opponent of the great capitalists whose aim it is to mobilise for themselves all agricultural values, and to oust the farmers by means of taxation and interest on loans, National Socialism demands State protection of the farmers against aggression by the big business interests. We need a strong, healthy class of farmers, free from the thraldom of interest and the tyranny of taxation.

II

The second question was addressed to me personally, as having been appointed by Hitler 'final arbiter of all questions touching the Programme'.

"What is the attitude of National Socialism towards inheritance of property, and succession duties?"

Answer. Since it is the mainstay of the national idea, continuity of ownership, i.e. inheritance of the land which a man's forefathers reclaimed and cultivated, is a natural consequence. National Socialism therefore recognises the principle of inheritance, as it does that of ownership of land.

If property goes to distant relatives the National Socialist State will levy a special tax, but in the case of nearer relationship this will be assessed at the rate prevailing at the moment.

III

This question was set owing to anxiety — quite unfounded — regarding the possible consequences of prohibiting loans from private capitalists on the security of the land.

Answer. A State, which desires to make agricultural property free from debt, and to rescue the farmers from the claws of professional financiers — so many farmers having been, as it is, driven from their homes by the Jews —, a State, which desires to break down the money monopoly of capitalism and to abolish the thraldom of interest, is not likely to withhold the necessary credits nor to charge extortionate interest; on the contrary, National Socialism intends to assist agriculture to the utmost.

1. The Policy of the N.S.D.A.P.

IV

"Breaking down the thraldom of interest." Abolition of unearned incomes. "What is the attitude of the National Socialist Party towards capital saved or inherited?"

Answer. Has any farmer today an 'unearned income' out of demands for interest, or can any landowner live on money saved from his rents?

This means that there is anxiety among certain land-owners who still have a little capital left, or else there is intentional miscomprehension or ignorance of that most essential demand of the National Socialist Programme.

N. B. We mean literally "breaking down the thraldom of interest". No one will describe small amounts of interest from savings or a mortgage or a government loan, as the thraldom of interest. What we mean by it is when deliberate inflation has robbed us of all our savings, and the farmer has to pay interest on fresh mortgages and short term credits at rates which ruin him.

Those who favour of sticking to the present system of capitalism are against the true interests of the farmers, and in favour of allowing the banks and their agents to batten on agriculture.

For the rest I would refer readers to my pamphlets entitled Der Staat auf nationaler und sozialer Grundlage, and Das Programm der N.S.D.A.P.

V

Our policy as regards taxation states clearly and consistently: To free the consumer from the burden of indirect taxation, and the producer from taxes which cramp his business.

"Does the Party intend to remove import duties?"

Answer. The Landbund ought to be aware that the National

Socialist vote in the Reichstag went absolutely in favour of protective duties on agricultural produce, in accordance with its principle — Protection of the nation's work in town and country.

VI

The question of Profit-sharing. It is impossible here to deal with this wide and difficult subject. In my weekly journal, Die Flamme, I have described our attitude in detail in a number of articles.

The article in the Deutsche Tageszeitung is misleading, since it removes from their context the sentences which it quotes. I personally consider that profit-sharing in the general sense of the capitalist and Marxist schools of ideas is not the correct solution. On this subject our Programme refers to workers in factories, and there is no point in attempting to clear up the question in a pamphlet dealing with agriculture.

VII

Extension of Old Age Insurance Benefits.

"How is it proposed to raise the funds for this purpose?"

Answer. There is provision now for Old Age Insurance, but it is in many cases insufficient, and is regarded as pauperisation. Once the burden of taxation is removed, and those who are now unemployed but able to work are restored to the economic sphere, there will be sufficient means for providing ample Old Age benefits for those who are past work.

VIII, IX, X

These are merely questions to do with Party tactics, and not with any principle.

Being in opposition against a coalition which has brought unhappiness to Germany, we have naturally now and again to vote with the Communists (although a whole world divides

1. The Policy of the N.S.D.A.P.

us from them), just as the German National and the Christian National Farmers do. We allow no one to dictate to us where we get our adherents from, but we turn to all — workers, bourgeois and farmers — who have a good German heart in their bodies and are men of good will, and desire to see an end of Parliamentary mis-government and the wretched policy of fulfilment (of the Peace Treaties). We do not consider that 'social communication' with other Parties is a proper method of freeing the German nation from Marxism and Parliamentarianism, — for that leads to political bargaining. Nothing but dictatorial action and determined exercise of power can pull Germany out of the mud.

The nation wants not fine words, but forcefulness; not bargaining, but solid work for our poor, down-trodden nation.

A full and clear account of the foregoing is given in No. 19 of the National Socialist collection — Unsertaglich Brot: Basic Questions of German Agriculture; by Hermann Schneider, Ekersdorf, Kreis Namslau, regarding the whole policy of National Socialism with respect to agriculture. It contains well conceived proposals for re-establishing the suffering farming class of Germany.

> No. 16, by Dr. Buchner, contains an excellent essay on the meaning and spirit of our economic policy.

> No 12, by Colonel Hierl, describes our policy of national defence.

We shall conclude with a few remarks on certain questions which our political enemies misrepresent spitefully and untruthfully in the hope of doing us an injury.

Our attitude towards the permanent official class is surely a worthy one. We should not be such whole-hearted admirers of the great King of Prussia if we were against this class. What the Army was abroad, a pure, incorruptible official class is for the State at home. Honour and duty must once again become essential qualities in our officials. The kind of officials, who are at the beck and call of the Reds and the Blacks, will disappear in the coming State; such Party wire-pullers have no use for honour and duty.

The suggestion that the National Socialists are against the officials and intend to reduce their pay and do away with pensions, is of the nature of a political lie, which has been circulated by the Press of our opponents. On the contrary, we desire to grant to all members of the nation who have served Germany faithfully all their lives long, a pension of honour which will relieve them of cares in their old age. It is only thus that social assistance will be freed from the stigma of 'pauperisation'.

We must also refer to the extension of the pension idea to the independent trades and hand-workers. There is no need to worry about how we are to raise funds for the purpose. When we cease paying thousands of millions abroad each year, and still more to our own banking houses, a fraction of those sums will suffice to pay for Old Age Pensions.

Unemployment Assistance and Insurance.

It is not, in itself, the affair of the State to support with State funds men who are able to work. Our attitude towards the present system of assistance for those who cannot earn a living has never altered; we have always pressed in Parliament for better conditions for the workless. This we do, not because we think it a right state of things, but because a Government like the present one, whose idiotic foreign and domestic policy has carried labour, food production and all commerce to the edge of the abyss, is in duty bound to let its policy go by the board.

A State which is unable to reinstate in the economic world millions of men who can work, deserves to be swept away; so if it fails financially to meet the problem of assistance to unemployment, we merely shrug our shoulders.

1. The Policy of the N.S.D.A.P.

The various attacks on the system of the dole, even if justified when they refer to cases of abuse of this social assistance, fail to turn us from the principle we believe in. Granted that, amongst nearly 3,000,000 unemployed there may be 2 or 300,000 notorious scrimshankers who would readily return to work if the dole were removed — we must not forget that there remain at least 2½ million good workers, employees, engineers, technicians, foremen, clerks, etc. seeking desperately for work and unable to find it. It is owing to the failure of our thoroughly unsound State policy that it is impossible to make any change in the miserable unemployed dole.

Attacks on Religion and the Clergy.

We cannot declare too often that the N.S.D.A.P. is not dreaming of attacking the Christian religion and its worthy servants.

It is the corrupting policy of the Centre and the Bavarian People's Party which we attack; these lose no opportunity of crying "Church in Danger" except when they are making common cause with the atheistical, God-denying Social Democracy.

It is because we have so high and holy an ideal of man's relation towards his God that we hate to see religion besmirched with the dirt of political conflict.

2. The 25 Points

The National Socialist German Workers' Party at a great mass meeting on February 25th, 1920, in the Hofbrauhous-Festsaal in Munich announced their Programme to the world. In section 2 of the Constitution of our Party this Programme is declared to be inalterable.

The Programme

The Programme of the German Workers' Party is limited as to period. The leaders have no intention, once the aims announced in it have been achieved, of setting up fresh ones, merely in order to increase the discontent of the masses artificially, and so ensure the continued existence of the Party.

1. We demand the union of all Germans to form a Great Germany on the basis of the right of the self-determination enjoyed by nations.

2. We demand equality of rights for the German People in its dealings with other nations, and abolition of the Peace Treaties of Versailles and St. Germain.

3. We demand land and territory (colonies) for the nourishment of our people and for settling our superfluous population.

4. None but members of the nation may be citizens of the State. None but those of German blood, whatever their creed, may be members of the nation. No Jew, therefore, may be a member of the nation.

5. Anyone who is not a citizen of the State may live in Germany only as a guest and must be regarded as being subject to foreign laws.

6. The right of voting on the State's government and legislation

The Programme of the N.S.D.A.P.

is to be enjoyed by the citizen of the State alone. We demand therefore that all official appointments, of whatever kind, whether in the Reich, in the country, or in the smaller localities, shall, be granted to citizens of the State alone.

We oppose the corrupting custom of Parliament of filling posts merely with a view to party considerations, and without reference to character or capability.

7. We demand that the State shall make it its first duty to promote the industry and livelihood of citizens of the State. If it not possible to nourish the entire population of the State, foreign nationals (non-citizens of the State) must be excluded from the Reich.

8. All non-German immigration must be prevented. We demand that all non-Germans, who entered Germany subsequent to August 2nd, 1914, shall be required forthwith to depart from the Reich.

9. All citizens of the State shall be equal as regards rights and duties.

10. It must be the first duty of each citizen of the State to work with his mind or with his body. The activities of the individual may not clash with the interests of the whole, but must proceed within the frame of the community and be for the general good.

We demand therefore:

11. Abolition of incomes unearned by work.

Abolition of the Thraldom of Interest

12. In view of the enormous sacrifice of life and property demanded of a nation by every war, personal enrichment due to a war must be regarded as a crime against the nation. We demand therefore ruthless confiscation of all war gains.

13. We demand nationalisation of all businesses which have been up to the present formed into companies (Trusts).

14. We demand that the profits from wholesale trade shall be shared out.

15. We demand extensive development of provision for old age.

16. We demand creation and maintenance of a healthy middle class, immediate communalisation of wholesale business premises, and their lease at a cheap rate to small traders, and that extreme consideration shall be shown to all small purveyors to the State, district authorities and smaller localities.

17. We demand land-reform suitable to our national requirements, passing of a law for confiscation without compensation of land for communal purposes; abolition of interest on land loans, and prevention of all speculation in land[25].

18. We demand ruthless prosecution of those whose activities are injurious to the common interest. Sordid criminals against the nation, usurers, profiteers, etc. must be punished

---

25 On April 13th, 1928, Adolf Hitler made the following declaration: It is necessary to reply to the false interpretation on the part of our opponents of Point 17 of the Programme of the N.S.D.A.P. Since the N.S.D.A.P. admits the principle of private property, it is obvious that the expression 'confiscation without compensation" merely refers to possible legal powers to confiscate, if necessary, land illegally acquired, or not administered in accordance with national welfare. It is directed in accordance with national welfare. It is directed in the first instance against the Jewish companies which speculate in land. Munich, April 13th, 1928. (signed) Adolf Hitler.

with death, whatever their creed or race.

19. We demand that the Roman Law, which serves the materialistic world order, shall be replaced by a legal system for all Germany.

20. With the aim of opening to every capable and industrious German the possibility of higher education and of thus obtaining advancement, the State must consider a thorough re-construction of our national system of education. The curriculum of all educational establishments must be brought into line with the requirements of practical life. Comprehension of the State idea (State sociology) must be the school objective, beginning with the first dawn of intelligence in the pupil. We demand development of the gifted children of poor parents, whatever their class or occupation, at the expense of the State.

21. The State must see to raising the standard of health in the nation by protecting mothers and infants, prohibiting child labour, increasing bodily efficiency by obligatory gymnastics and sports laid down by law, and by extensive support of clubs engaged in the bodily development of the young.

22. We demand abolition of a paid army and formation of a national army.

23. We demand legal warfare against conscious political lying and its dissemination in the Press. In order to facilitate creation of a German national Press we demand:

    (a) that all editors of newspapers and their assistants, employing the German language, must be members of the nation;

    (b) that special permission from the State shall be necessary before non-German newspapers may appear. These are not necessarily printed in the German language;

(c) that non-Germans shall be prohibited by law from participation financially in or influencing German newspapers, and that the penalty for contravention of the law shall be suppression of any such newspaper, and immediate deportation of the non-German concerned in it.

It must be forbidden to publish papers which do not conduce to the national welfare. We demand legal prosecution of all tendencies in art and literature of a kind likely to disintegrate our life as a nation, and the suppression of institutions which militate against the requirements above-mentioned.

24. We demand liberty for all religions denominations in the State, so far as they are not a danger to it and do not militate against the moral feelings of the German race.

The Party, as such, stands for positive Christianity, but does not bind itself in the matter of creed to any particular confession. It combats the Jewish-materialist spirit within us and without us, and is convinced that our nation can only achieve permanent health from within on the principle:

The Common Interest Before Self

25. That all the foregoing may be realised we demand the creation of a strong central power of the State. Unquestioned authority of the politically centralised Parliament over the entire Reich and its organisation: and formation of Chambers for classes and occupations for the purpose of carrying out the general laws promulgated by the Reich in the various States of the confederation. The leaders of the Party swear to go straight forward — if necessary to sacrifice their lives — in securing fulfilment of the foregoing Points.

After full discussion at the General Meeting of members on May

22nd, 1920, it was resolved that "This Programme is unalterable". This does not imply that every word must stand unchanged, nor that anything done to deepen or develop the Programme is to be prohibited, but it implies with absolute decision and unswerving clarity that the principles and leading ideas contained in it may not be tampered with. There can be no bending or twisting from considerations of expediency, no hidden interference with very important — and for the present-day arrangements in politics, society and economics, very unwelcome —-points in the Programme, no deviation of sentiment.

Adolf Hitler prints its two main points in leaded type:

- The Common Interest before Self — the spirit of the Programme.

- Abolition of the Thraldom of Interest — the core of National Socialism.

Once these two points are achieved, it means a victory of the approaching universalist ordering of society in the 'true State' over the present-day separation of State, nation and economics under the corrupting influence of the individualist theory of society as now constructed. The sham State of today, oppressing the working classes and protecting the pirated gains of bankers and Stock Exchange speculators, is the arena for reckless private enrichment and for the lowest political profiteering; it gives no thought to its people, and provides no high moral bond of union. The power of money, most ruthless of all powers, holds absolute control, and exercises corrupting, destroying influence on State, nation, society, morals, drama, literature, and on all matters of morality, less easy to estimate.

There must of course be no wavering, no drawing back in this giant struggle; it is either victory or defeat.

The somewhat varied view of the same basic principle, which I

2. The 25 Points

gave in my book, Der deutsche Staat auf nationaler und sozialer Grundlage, (F. Eher Nachf.) is not an alteration, but a series of points which belong together, collected and arranged according to various political economic, financial, and cultural, aspects of life.

If those views of mine could be looked on as varying from or opposed to the 25 Points, Hitler would never have described my book in his brief preface as the "catechism of our movement". Anyone is free to choose either of the views according to his taste, but if he compares them together he will not find them mutually contradictory.

In order to insure for the future absolute agreement in our demands as expressed in our Programme, and to guard the movement against the shocks likely to injure any movement, — the 'suggestions for improvement' offered by professional and amateur critics, grumblers and know-alls, Adolf Hitler, at a conference of all district organisers held at Bamberg on February 14th, 1926, formally appointed Gottfried Feder to be the final judge of all questions connected with the Programme.

3. The Basic Ideas

It is our intention in this pamphlet to expose the essential principles of the National Socialist conception of the State as briefly and simply as possible. We shall in a later one deal in more detail with the sociological, theoretic and spiritual aspects of that conception.

We shall also not attempt to describe the various other political aspirations nor those who represent them in the different parties and associations — this is a task by itself —, but we set down here merely the essential points of our demands.

The world arose out of chaos, order out of disorder, organisation out of wild confusion.

Today chaos is rampant in the world, — confusion, struggle, hatred, oppression, robbery, cruelty, self-seeking. Brother is estranged from brother. Members of the same nation attack each other, stab a man to death simply because he wears a Swastika Cross. They all suffer under the same burdens, the same privations; yet who ever during these last months has heard of Marxist workers attacking or killing their employers, or their party leaders, or any of the bankers and Stock Exchange bloodsuckers, or any of the wholesale profiteers? The sole sacrifice to chaos is the good, simple worker. The Marxists have lost their heads and are crowding to join up with the plunderers of their own class, whilst they turn savagely against those who stand ready to rescue it.

The Nationalist and other Parties are in the Government, or are fighting to get into it with those who have destroyed their national ideals, and lose thereby both honour and character. The defence associations are striving to penetrate 'into the State' — the State of Severing and Grzesinsky, — pacifists, internationalists and Jews, with whom they believe they can run the government.

They have gone off their heads! The so-called Rechtskreise fail to see that eagles and snakes, wolves and lambs, mankind and the cholera bacillus, cannot join in co-operation. They are putting forth all their strength to give an appearance of 'order' to disorder, political chaos, political effeteness. But they set their faces against the National Socialists, those 'fanatics', being filled with crazy fears that the latter might deprive them of some of their former privileges and positions, — forgetting that they lost all through the very people from whom they now demand a share in the political loaves and fishes.

The industrials, great or small, have but one end in view — profits —, only one longing — credits —, only one protest — against taxation; they fear and respect only one thing — the banks; they shrug their shoulders over the National Socialist demand for breaking down the thraldom of interest.

Their one desire is to 'make debts'. The vast tribute extracted from loans by the banks, without trouble or labour, they regard as perfectly in order. They found parties of economy and vote for the Dawes Laws, which are the main cause of the heavy taxation.

Honour has departed from business, which is all in the hands of powerful companies. The producers have surrendered to high finance, their greatest enemy. The employers in the factories and offices, deep in debt, have to be content with the barest pittance, for all the profits of labour go into the pockets of the impersonal money power in the form of interest and dividends.

The people in control are totally unable to stem the chaos. Crushed from above by taxation and interest payment, menaced from below by the grumblings of the submerged workers, they have, bound themselves blindly to a State controlled by

3. The Basic Ideas

capitalism, whilst the exploiters of the present chaos suffer them to remain in power merely as slavedrivers over the labouring masses. Their fury is directed not against the lunacy of Marxism, but against the wearers of the Hooked Cross. They forget that we and we alone saw the tragedy of German economics approaching, perceived and showed how, if taken in time, Germany by her own strength could restore the balance.

Associations under every kind of name, reasonable in their basic ideas — hopeless in the present chaos of public life, are seeking how to produce order. It is all in vain, for they are not in touch with the nation as a great social whole. All are merely intent on snatching small advantages for their own caste; bare of any political or economic principle, they apply to each political party in turn. They bow to the existing system and kow-tow to the so-called supreme authority.

They cost the German nation untold sums in payments to numberless organisers, directors and wire-pullers, but no one of them does the least good. Inflation — a criminal measure — robbed all classes, the thrifty, members of associations, artizans of their savings. Some new tax, straight from the green table, destroys the hopes based on years of work. An advantage gained after numberless meetings, discussions, deputations to the Government, is usually annulled by a rise in the cost of living, or a rise or a fall in prices.

Chaos and lunacy! How can a farmer live under such persecution? How can the worker buy with prices rising all the time? What good is it to raise the pay of officials and employees when the index of the cost of living continues to rise. They look in their credulity for help from the State, the State which has caused all the impoverishment and suppression, which is not the 'Father of the Nation', but the tyrant and tax-collector of the money despotism.

So they turn again and again to the old Parties, say they don't care for politics and belong to no Party, and at the same time let the wretched Party squabbles go on as before.

The Programme of the N.S.D.A.P.

The great task which National Socialism has set before it is a determination to restore form, to dispel the chaos, to set the world, which has departed from the old dispensations, in order again, and to guard that order — in the highest Platonic sense.

It should be stated here that we regard as 'Order' neither the apparent order of a policed State, nor the robbery of finance hallowed by custom and permitted by law, nor the conspiracies of syndicates, trusts, and other organised measures of national betrayal, however well they 'function'. Even a band of robbers has 'order', prisons have their 'regulations'. But in the nation, taken as an organic whole, every aspect of our public life shows pain, bondage, suppression, insincerity, and presents a chaotic picture of a struggle of all against all.

Government against people, Party against Party, at the same time concluding most unnatural alliances, employer against employee, merchant against producer and consumer, landlord against tenant, labourer against farmer, officials against the public, worker against 'bourgeoisie', Church against State, each blindly hitting out at his particular adversary and thinking only of his own selfish interests, his advancement and his money-bags. No one reflects that the other has a right to live, or that pursuit of his own selfish ends means that someone else has to pay for it. No one thinks of his neighbour's welfare, or of his higher duties to the community. A breathless pursuit after personal gain. Elbow your neighbour to get on, tramp on his body if you will get anything by it — why care? That is modern business.

Let us not deceive ourselves. We are in the midst of a great world change, and it is natural that simple souls, poor wandering spirits, see no way out of the chaos, seek relief in suicide, or think the world is coming to an end and join in the race after the golden calf and rush blindly into the whirlpool. "Enjoy while you can — after us the deluge."

3. The Basic Ideas

So terrible a blow to the morale of a nation is only possible and explicable when the whole intellectual foundation of society is shaken or else false, — and in fact we see that Marxism, Capitalism, and the leaders of our public life all worship the same god — Individualism. Personal interest is the sole incentive, — obtaining advantages for one's own narrow class in life.

Later on a further contribution to this series will appear, devoted to a careful sociological study of the construction of society.

Here I shall only attempt shortly to show a comparative picture of the difference between the organic errors in the State and political economy of today and the essence of a National Socialist State. The present day doctrine is: Society is the sum of the individuals — the State at its best a convenient aggregation of individuals or associations

We may compare this doctrine of the construction of society to a heap of stones. The only real thing about it is the individual pieces of stone. Its shape is a matter of chance; whether a stone is on top or underneath is indifferent. The result is neither more nor less than a heap of stones.

By the same simile, the State which answers to our National Socialist doctrine of society and philosophy of the State is the house. Speaking mechanically, the house also consists of so many individual bricks — sand, cement, joists, windows, doors, floors, etc. But any one can see that a house, a room, is a higher entity, something new and peculiar and complete in itself, more than a mere sum total of bricks heaped together. Any one can understand that a house does not come into being by piling a number of single parts in a heap, but only by assembling these parts according to a deliberate plan.

Thus it is with a nation. Not until chaos has been organically, by a deliberate plan, brought into order and gives place to form, not until a reasoned whole has been assembled out of the mass of parts, can the true State appear. Only then will the component parts assume a purposeful shape. Othmar Spann, formerly Rector of Vienna University, has explained admirably in his book, Derwahre Staat, and in his Gesellschaftslehre the sociological bases of the present day individualistic State as opposed to the high ideal of universal order in a State founded on scientific principles.

We National Socialists coined the phrase, which all men can comprehend:

The Community Before the Individual

It is only by serving the general interest as a member of the national community that the individual awakes to a higher life, each one in his own place. Only so will each one attain to the genuine Socialism, the communal feeling, the true life, win consciousness of security, and realise that only under the domination of this idea can an organic, national government arise from the present day system of robbery, and be of profit to the community, and to each member of the community.

Today the individual is a helpless victim of the forces fighting for the mastery; his associations are powerless to help him. It is not clearly realised who is the real enemy — the idle profiteer and exploiter.

In spite of the Marxist cry against capitalism, the pious pronouncements of the Centre, the complaints of the business world about the burden of taxation and interest, no one realises the world enemy, the finance which overshadows the world, and its representative, the Jewish magnate.

All classes have felt the lash of interest; the tax collector bears heavy on every section of the population, — but who dares oppose the power of bank and Stock Exchange? Capital proclaims its character by growing, contrary to all experience elsewhere on earth, as it were outside itself without pains or labour, by means

3. The Basic Ideas

of interest and dividends, and by waxing greater and more powerful each minute. The devilish principle of lies has bested the decency of creative labour.

Break down the thraldom of interest is our war-cry.

I know that this demand, which underlies every other, is not properly understood in its full vast significance even in our own ranks. Very few of our speakers, for instance, dare to attack this basic question, though most of them feel how important it is; for one of our Party slogans is "Fight capital and the Stock Exchange". But what the 'thraldom of interest' really is, how it bears on the life of the nation and the individual, how 'finance' has enslaved the population, and what the right and practical methods are which must be adopted to break it, and what the results of breaking it would be for the whole population — is sufficiently clear to very few to enable them to explain it in ther own words.

In his great work, Mein Kampf, (Vol I, pp. 224—225) Adolf Hitler has indicated the vast importance of this question as follows:

"As I listened to Gottfried Feder's first lecture on breaking down the thraldom of interest in June, 1919, I knew at once that this was a theoretic truth immensely important for the future of the German nation . . . The fight against international capital and finance has become the chief point in the Programme for the German nation's struggle for independence and liberty:'

All serious National Socialists share this conviction, for the solution of this question implies solution of the Jewish question, — and much more than that.

Anti-semitism is in a way the foundation of the feeling underlying our whole movement. Every National Socialist is an anti-Semite, but every anti-semite need not be a National Socialist. Anti-semitism is negative; the anti-semite recognises the carrier of the national plague, but this knowledge usually turns into hatred of the individual Jew and the success of the Jews in the life of business. Then in the best event anti-semitism rises up to help in driving the Jew out of our State and economic life. The anti-semite does not worry his head about How and What next.

If, even after the Jew was driven out, there still remained the principle of present-day Jewish domination — self-interest before general interest — and the Jewish banking and credit system, there would still be enough bastard Jews, or even 'normal Germans' of mixed race as ready to step into the Jews' shoes and rage against their own race as are the Jews today, and we should perhaps see plenty of 'anti-semites' sitting where the Jews once sat.

Now National Socialism with its main demand, Breaking down the Thraldom of Interest, is essentially constructive. It bites deeper, and the consequences are far more all-embracing.

In my essay, Das Herzstück unseres Programms, (Nat.Soc. Jahrbuch, 1927) I pointed to the peculiar position that demand gives us among all other Parties and associations. In all our other demands we find similar and parallel aspirations in the Parties of the Right and Left. No other Party but ourselves can show any counterpart of this one demand.

We all know that neither the Left, with their false cry of "Down with Capitalism", nor the Right with their phrases about the Fatherland, are capable of starting a new world epoch, for neither the Marxists nor the reactionaries could alter anything in the nature of our economy but would only destroy as the Communists in Russia do. They are incapable of construction — like the Communists in Russia.

3. The Basic Ideas

What Do We Mean by Thraldom of Interest?

The condition of peoples under the money domination of the finance of the world Jewry.

The land-owner is under this thraldom, who has to raise loans to finance his farming operations, — loans at such high interest as almost to eat up the results of his labour —, or who is forced to make debts and to drag the mortgages after him like so much, weight of lead.

So is the worker, producing in shops and factories for a pittance, whilst the shareholder draws dividends and bonuses which he has not worked for.

So is the earning middle class, whose work goes almost entirely to pay the interest on bank overdrafts.

So are all who must earn their bread by mental or bodily work, whilst a comparatively small proportion, without labour or trouble, pocket huge profits out of their dividends, speculations and bank shares.

We do not refer to the thrifty savers and small capitalists — though they too owe, or owed, their winnings to a false system —, but all their lives long many of times the amount of their little interest was taken from them in the form of taxes, so that we can easily afford to repay them in their old age a part of their full earnings, which were taken away. I shall have more to say about this later on.

So is the industrialist, who has labouriously built up his business, and turned it in course of time into a company. He is no longer a free agent, but has to satisfy the greedy board of directors and his shareholders as well — if he does not wish to be squeezed out. So are all nations that cover their deficits by means of loans.

This thraldom spells ruin for any nation that hands over to

the money power, the bankers, its sovereign rights at home, the control of its finances, of its railways, and of taxation and customs, as Germany has done by accepting the Dawes Law.

Creative labour is under the same thraldom, if it thinks of money before all else. Today money, the 'servant of business', has become the master, in fact, the brutal tyrant of labour.

Thraldom of interest is the real expression for the antagonisms, Capital versus Labour, blood versus money, creative work versus exploitation. The necessity of breaking this thraldom is of such vast importance for our nation and our race, that on it alone depends our nation's hope of rising up from its shame and slavery; in fact, the hope of recovering happiness, prosperity and civilisation throughout the world.

"It is the pivot on which everything turns; it is far more than a mere-necessity of financial policy. Whilst its principles and consequences bite deep into political and economic life, it is a leading question for economic study, and thus affects every single individual and demands a decision from each one: — Service to the nation or unlimited private enrichment. It means a solution of the Social Question."

All 'world-questions' are capable of being described in one word, which rises like a flame out of chaos; at the same time countless prophets and books cannot exhaust all the questions which arise out of that word.

We can say no more at present on this vast basic principle of National Socialism. I have already thrown light on every essential side of the problem in my pamphlets: *Das Manifest zur Brechung der Zinsknechtschaft* — Munich, 1926 ; *Der Staatsbankrott, Die Rettung* — Jos. C. Huber, Diessen, 1919; *Der kommende Steuerstreik* — Diessen, 1921; and *Der Deutsche Staat auf nationaler und sozialer Grundlage* — Frz. Eher Nachf., Munich.

3. The Basic Ideas

Intensive study is required to master the details of this problem, for the practical economics of the last 50 years have followed the capitalistic idea so closely, that all who have grown up with it need a complete change of orientation in order to get free from it.

A pamphlet on the subject is soon to appear, which will give our members an explanation on this highly important task of the coming nationalist State.

In addition to the two quite novel basic principles of our Programme given above, we must mention certain others in connection with the general policy of the State.

The principle underlying our policy of the State is shortly as follows: The German Reich is the home of the Germans.

It is the great principle for our whole foreign policy, and includes Germany's political liberation, all the requirements of our racial policy, and the conditions of membership of the State.

Our economic principle is: The duty of the national economy is to provide the necessities of life and not to secure the highest possible profits for capital.

This principle of economic policy embraces a fundamental attitude of National Socialism towards private property, and with regard to the various forms of business, from the very small to the very great — Syndicates, Trusts — and also to the great moral questions which must be a living force in business, if the 'national economics' are not to sink to being mere exploitation of the nation and to being run simply for profit!

Our principle as regards finance is as follows: Finance shall exist for the benefit of the State; the financial magnates shall not form a State within the State.

This principle involves a seismic change. It concerns the practical measures which will have to be taken to break the Thraldom of Interest, — nationalisation of finance, control of the system of credit, and the banking system.

Every one of these tasks is of the greatest importance from the point of view of our Programme. They involve all tax legislation, with the ultimate — and seemingly impossible — aim of a State without taxation.

Our principle as regards social subjects is as follows:

The General Welfare is the Highest Law of All

This principle of ours is in direct opposition to present day practice, according to which every class, every profession, tries to win advantages for its own particular group in social policy without regard to the general interest. We wish to make it possible for all to find a dwelling and for all to make a living, and to institute a general system of care for the aged.

As regards educational and moral progress it is our unchangeable principle: that all work in that direction is to be done from the sole point of view of German nationality. It cannot be by order or by force that the moral and intellectual forces of our nation may introduce a new Renaissance, a new classic epoch in the arts. A stop will have to be put to the injuries suffered by our German artistic and intellectual life at the hands of the Jewish dictatorship, especially through the poisoning of the press.

Apart from this important domain of public life there are, of course, plenty of other improvements to be considered.

It is clear that our system of Law will have to be modified to meet the variety of fresh institutions; that the scandal of election to Parliament by the democratic vote will have to be removed, and that, following the transitional period of a Dictatorship, we shall have to decide on the outward visible form of the State and

3. The Basic Ideas

the internal functions of the federal States.

Already, however, we can see in this brief outline the vast dimensions of these questions when set face to face with the tremendous fundamental principles of our Programme.

It is not fundamental — in fact it is indifferent to us whether is to be a monarchy or a republic, whether we are to have a federation of 5 or 25 States, provided only they are all German States combined under a strong central government, when face to face with the foreigner, and provided only the citizens of the German State at home may live happy and contented.

4. The Programme Requirements In Detail

As Formulated by Gottfried Feder
In Der Deutsche Staat.

It will make for clarity, when enlisting new members, to make use of the Programme in the form which follows. The minor clauses are arranged under the more important headings, corresponding to the principles outlined in the preceding chapter.

The Political and Economic
Programme of the N.S.D.A.P.

Our aim is Germany's rebirth to German liberty in the German spirit. The means to this aim are:

I. The political principle: The German Reich is the home of the Germans.

(a) in foreign policy:

1. Formation of a homogeneous national State, embracing all of German race.

2. Energetic representation of German interests abroad.

(b) in racial policy:

3. Dismissal of all Jews and non-Germans from all responsible positions in public life.

4. Prevention of immigration of Eastern Jews and other parasitic foreigners. Undesirable foreigners and Jews to be deported.

(c) in internal policy:

5. None but Germans who profess entire community with the

spirit and destiny of Germany may exercise the rights of a citizen of the State.

6. He who is not a German may only live in the German State as a guest and is under foreign law.

7. The rights of Germans shall have the preference over those of citizens of foreign nations.

II. Our economic principle: The duty of the State is to provide the necessities of life and not to secure the highest possible profits for capital.

8. National Socialism recognises private property as a principle and protects it by law.

9. The national welfare however demands that a limit shall be set to the amassing of wealth in the hands of individuals.

10. All Germans form a community for the promotion of the general welfare and Kultur.

11. Within the limits of the obligation of every German to work, the sanctity of private property being respected, every German is free to earn and to dispose of the results of his labour.

12. The healthy combination of all forms of business, small and large, in every domain of economic life, including agriculture, shall be encouraged.

13. All existing businesses which until now have been in the form of companies shall be nationalised.

14. Usury and profiteering and personal enrichment at the expense and to the injury of the nation shall be punished with death.

4. The Programme Requirements In Detail

15. Introduction of a year's obligation to work (for the State), incumbent on every German.

III. Our financial principle: Finance shall exist for the benefit of the State; the financial magnates shall not form a State within the State. Hence our aim to break the thraldom of interest.

16. Relief of the State, and hence of the nation, from its indebtedness to the great financial houses which lend on interest.

17. Nationalisation of the Reichsbank and the issuing houses.

18. Provision of money for all great public objects (waterpower, railroads, etc.), not by means of loans, but by granting non-interest bearing State bonds or without using ready money.

19. Introduction of a fixed standard of currency on a secured basis.

20. Creation of a national bank of business development (currency reform) for granting non-interest bearing loans.

21. Fundamental re-modelling of the system of taxation on social-economic principles. Relief of the consumer from the burden of indirect taxation, and of the producer from crippling taxation (fiscal reform and relief from taxation).

IV. Our social-political principle: The general welfare is the highest law of all.

22. Development on a large scale of Old Age Insurance by nationalising the system of annuities, Every member of the German State shall be assured of enough to live upon on attaining a certain age, or, if permanently disabled, before that age.

The Programme of the N.S.D.A.P.

23. Participation by all engaged in productive enterprises in the profits according to efficiency and age. Responsibility will also be shared in fulfilling the task from a national point of view.

24. Seizure for social purposes of all profits made out of the War and the Revolution, not due to honest work, and of the fortunes of usurers and money-grabbers.

25. Relief of the shortage of dwellings by extensive fresh construction throughout the Reich by the means suggested in No. 20. (a new national bank).

V. Our cultural aim is that all the sciences and fine arts shall flourish on the basis of a politically free, and economically healthy State.

The means of achieving this will be:

26. Training the young up to be healthy in body and free in mind, after the great traditions of German culture.

27. Complete liberty of creed and conscience.

28. Special protection for the Christian denominations.

29. Discouragement of dogmas, which are opposed to German moral instincts and contain matter injurious to the State and the nation.

30. Discouragement of all evil influences in the press, in literature, the stage, the arts and the picture theatres.

31. Liberty of instruction in the German secondary schools; formation of a ruling class of high-minded men.

VI. Military affairs.

4. The Programme Requirements In Detail

32. To make the nation efficient by permitting every free German to serve and bear arms.

33. Abolition of the paid Army.

34. Creation of a national Army for national defence under the command of a highly trained corps of professional officers.

VII. Other recommendations.

35. Press reform. Suppression of all journals which militate against the national good. Strict responsibility for all untrue and intentionally falsified intelligence.

36. Modification of the franchise laws so as to cut out the demoralising methods of election contests, and the immunity of those elected.

37. Formation of special Chambers for trades and professions.

38. Judicial reform as regards: the Land Laws — recognisation of the rights of property in land as a principle; no right to borrow from private sources on the security of the land; the State to have the right of pre-emption, especially in the case of foreigners and Jews; the State to be empowered to administer estates in the event of bad management on the part of the owner.

    Civil Law — greatly increased protection for personal honour, health, as opposed to the one-sided legal protection of the rights of property, which predominates at the present day.

39. State Law reform.

    The form of State most suitable to the German character is sovereign control united in a central personal power. The nation must decide later on whether this central personal power shall be wielded by an elected monarch or a president.

The Federal Character of the Reich

The constitution of the German nation out of a number of countries closely bound together by race and history makes it necessary that each one of the States shall be very extensively independent in internal affairs.

It is the affair of the Reich to represent the German nation abroad, and to provide for passports, customs, also for the Army and Navy.

There are three main obstacles to carrying out this national Programme of National Socialism: Marxism, the Parliamentary system, and the capitalist magnates.

1. Our anti-Marxist campaign is directed against the disruptive doctrines of the Jew, Karl Marx — that of the class-war which splits up the nation, that of destruction of private property which makes business impossible — and against the whole economic materialistic view of history.

2. Our campaign against parliaments is directed against the lack of responsibility of the so-called representatives of the people, who — being immune — can never be summoned in practice to answer for the results of their decisions; also against all the evils which arise out of the system (moral corruption, nepotism, venality), all resulting in the final evil — a government which is dependent on such a parliament.

3. Our campaign against Mammon, which ranks above the other two, is directed against the world-embracing power of money, i.e. the perpetual exploitation of our nation by the great lending houses.

It is also a tremendous struggle against the soul-killing, materialist spirit of greed and rapacity with all its disruptive accompaniments throughout our public, commercial and cultural life. The main battle is one between two world-theories, represented by two essentially differing structures — the spirit which has created

4. The Programme Requirements In Detail

and is creative and the unquiet, grasping spirit. The creative spirit, deep-rooted, but superior to the rest of the world in spiritual experience, is carried mainly by the Arian race; — The grabbing spirit, without roots anywhere, aiming only at material things, commercial, is chiefly represented by the Jews.

National Socialism, like anti-semitism, regards the Jewish-materialistic spirit as the chief cause of the evil; it knows however that this greatest struggle in history must not stop short at merely destroying the Semitic spirit; which is why the great Programme of National Socialism goes far beyond the anti-semitic desire to destroy, for it offers a positive constructive picture, showing how the National Socialist State of labour and achievement ought to appear when completed.

Once this high aim is achieved the National Socialist Party will dissolve automatically; for National Socialism will then be the entire life of the whole German nation. The N.S.D.A.P. is not a political Party in the ordinary sense of the word, but is that section of the nation, which is confident and sure of the future, which has gathered round strong and determined leaders to deliver Germany from shame and impotence abroad and from demoralisation at home, and to make her once again strong and respected abroad, and morally and economically healthy at home.

The German Reich Is the Home of the German People

Every word of this principle of State policy is a cut with a lash, when we consider the miserable state of things today.

The 'German Reich' — where is there a German Reich today? Can Germany lay claim to be called an independent State? No! Not even the most complacent pundits in State Law could describe a country, such as Germany is now, as one in full enjoyment of all its rights of sovereignty.

The five most important rights of a State are: sovereignty over

The Programme of the N.S.D.A.P.

its territory, its army, its finances, its internal administration and communications, and lastly its justice. You have only to put the matter in this way to any layman without further explanation of a nation's rights under International Law, and compare it with Germany's position today, and it becomes clear that it is impossible to maintain that a sovereign 'German Reich' exists any longer.

Our control of our territory is a mockery, for whenever France chooses she can seize upon German land without asking leave and without suffering opposition. Czechs, Poles, Danes can venture on any inroad into German territory without fear of hindrance. The 'accursed old regime' put a very different interpretation on the slightest breach of frontier. A military inroad into German territory then implied a 'state of war'.

To protect its territorial sovereignty a nation needs an armed force capable to repelling any attack on its land, and therefore on the lives and happiness of its nationals. A free State cannot permit a foreign Power to scrutinise its actions, or to have the right of deciding the strength, equipment, armaments, garrisons of its Army; if it does, it is certainly not 'sovereign'; it cannot command its means of power; it has given up control of its military forces. Germany has done this by giving in to the enemy Commissions for Disarmament and Control. Germany had already suffered this humiliation under the Armistice conditions, and had lost her international rights.

Nevertheless she might have retained some part of her internal control; but as soon as the military control was destroyed, the financial magnates seized the opportunity for limitless exploitation of German labour.

First of all the muddy torrent of Revolution burst forth over Germany; then the usurers and profiteers, the Social-democratic traitors, sons of chaos, deserters, jail-birds shared the power with the Democrats and Centre, and behind and over all the financiers, the Jews, did their business. Soon the Free Masons of the so-

4. The Programme Requirements In Detail

called National Parties, especially Brother Stresemann, were called in. The final blow was soon to come. The experts with their Dawes Law robbed Germany of control of her finances, which was bartered away to a handful of Jews, the German and foreign financial magnates. The Reichstag let the railways go, and with them all control of communications, also a great part of the control of taxation and customs, by handing them over to the Reparations Commissioner.

Control of justice hardly exists any more. The occupied districts are under foreign military law; special regulations govern the rest of Germany, such as those for the defence of the Republic; insecurity of rights, organised public robbery through the so-called Aufwertungsgesetze, forcing the Courts to declare that wrong is right. Germany is no longer a sovereign State. She is a colony of slaves. Germans are oppressed, thrown into prison, denied free speech — simply because they are still 'German' and desire to end their slavery.

Yes, we want to have Germany free again, and this coming German Reich shall be the home of the Germans, — not merely a machine for keeping order, not merely a 'State', an 'authority', a 'government', a sinecure for a handful of reigning houses, but a Home, that word of charm — love of home, lovely, sunny, beloved. The smell of the home earth rises up, the wanderer thrills with joy to feel the home soil beneath his feet; he is bound to it by blood ties. The home feeling is the feeling of security, and from that blossoms the fine flower of love of home. The State and nation can have no finer aim than this.

It greater than a cautious social policy, than unemployment insurance, than housing schemes, though indeed having one's own home is one of the strongest incentives for love of home.

Home is more than an 'Imperial State', which one serves, whether from enthusiasm or under compulsion.

It is more than an administration, more than the defence of one's own interests, more than a crib for cattle, or protection for person and property. All these public objects must serve the conception of home. Just as the idea of home has a special charm of the children in a properly organised family, as one's own room arouses very different feelings from a room in a hotel or a prison cell; home is something unspeakably tender and yet powerful, superior to the idea of an association for a purpose, which is the Liberal — parliamentary — democratic conception of the social State.

Policy of the State

Principle: The German Reich shall be a home for the Germans—not for Jews, Russians (Communists), Social Democrats, who have no fatherland called Germany (Crispien), nor for all the foreigners who make a longer or shorter stay on German soil. We are in sharp and fundamental opposition to the Weimar Constitution, which speaks only of 'German nationals', but ignores the conception of 'German' in the national, or rather racial, sense.

Each of the seven following theses has three separate aspects (a) foreign policy, (b) population, (c) citizenship.

A   Foreign policy.

1. Creation of a solid national State, embracing all branches of the German race.

All of German blood, whether living under French, Danish, Polish, Czech or Italian sovereignty, shall be united in a German Reich. We demand neither less nor more than what was demanded for our enemies — the right of Germans to decide to belong to their motherland, the German State.

We claim all Germans in Sudeten Germany, Alsace-Lorraine. Poland, the League colony of Austria, and the States which succeeded to the old Austria. This demand however expressly

4. The Programme Requirements In Detail

excludes any tendency towards imperialism; it is the simple and natural demand, which any strong nationality puts forward as its natural requirement.

2. Strong representation of German interests abroad is a further and necessary corollary of Point 1.

It is usually the best, most industrious and venturesome — engineers, explorers, professors, merchants, doctors — who go into foreign lands, carrying German Kultur with them. They are members of the great German national family, to which they must never be lost. They have a right to expect protection from home when they are abroad. They should be not merely disseminators of Kultur, but the conscious advance guard of the Germanic idea in the world; not 'apostles of humanity', but bearers of the Nordic idea.

Those who represent Germany abroad should not acquire foreign notions, but stick to their superior German character.

Our Foreign Office must be swept clean with an iron besom. We must finish with the obsequiousness towards the foreigner after the manner of Erzberger and Stresemann, and it will be seen that strong representation of German interests will be quite otherwise respected, and attention to German desires in place of contempt will be the result.

B   Racial policy.

3. Exclusion of Jews and all non-Germans from all responsible positions in public life.

This demand is so natural to us National Socialists that no further explanation is needed; but it is not possible to give convincing arguments in brief to those who fail to take in the principles of our racial doctrine. Anyone who looks on a Jew as a 'citizen of the State of the Jewish religion' — and not as a heterogeneous, segregated people, parasitic in character, will fail to appreciate the essentialness of this demand. If a man were to say or think that a cabbage which had grown by chance in the middle of a strawberry plant was a strawberry plant, and that good strawberries could be got from it, he would be as wrong as if he thought that a lion cub which had got in among a flock of sheep thereby became a sheep. A German would not be good as a government official in China or India, and we should not like to have a Chinaman or a Hottentot as a Treasury official or Mayor of a German town. And yet it would be better to have an Enver Pasha or a Chang Kai Chek in control in Germany than to have a Jew with free play for his disintegrating racial characteristics. What is certain is that the Revolution loosened the bands of order in the State, and that the long-established Jewish bankers, as well as the Jews from the East who have recently immigrated into Germany, have enriched themselves by impoverishing Germany. We have all seen and had experience of this; it has always been going on, this disintegration of Nordic institutions.

"There is but one way open for this crafty people, — it has nothing to hope for so long as order is maintained." (Goethe at the fair at Plundersweilen.) Therefore we demand:

4. That the immigration of Eastern Jews and other parasitic aliens shall be stopped, and that undesirable aliens and Jews shall be deported.

At the time of the great inflation Jews from Galicia and Poland flocked like vermin into the towns of Germany. Though there was great dearth of houses they soon were very well housed, whilst Germans had to creep into holes. They started their dirty business, buying up everything — pearls, Persian carpets, diamonds, gold, silver, platinum, War Loans, thousand mark notes, copper, lead, literature, theatres, grain (the Evaporator Company). They quickly became visibly rich, — and took rank as Germans — in the eyes of 'normal Germans'.

4. The Programme Requirements In Detail

Compromise is utterly inadmissible in meeting the case. We must have administrators whose racial beliefs are clear and unbending. The health of the race must be restored by practical application of the anti-semitic treatment, and our nation must be turned Northward in the sense of the Nordic idea.

This question does not perhaps belong properly to the 'provisional Programme' of the N.S.D.A.P.; but we must all understand clearly that not much can be done with the German nation until it has been 'de-bastardised'.

But we can state here and now that the terrible racial decadence has only — at any rate in theory — been stemmed, because of the remarkable interest aroused generally by questions of race and by there being a number of books on the subject; nothing however but solid and continuous work can allow us to make real progress.

C As regards State citizenship we demand:

5. That none but Germans, who believe in German Kultur and the common destiny of all Germans, shall enjoy the rights of a citizen of the State.

Even here limits must be drawn. People, who, even though German born, act consciously in a way injurious to the nation and the State, and receive and obey orders from abroad — i. e. do not accept a share in the common destiny, may not be allowed the rights of citizenship; there are plenty to whom we shall have to deny the high honour of enjoying these rights.

6. Non-Germans may only dwell in the German State as guests, and shall be regarded as being subject to foreign law.

This is a necessary principle, calculated to put an end forever to the eternal obsequiousness towards the foreigner. But it does not mean that we shall not welcome citizens of a foreign country warmly and treat them well as guests so long as they conduct themselves properly; but

7. The rights and interests of Germans shall have preference over those of the subjects of a foreign nation.

Our further requirements need not be included in our Programme in detail. For instance, the form assumed by the laws affecting foreigners will come on for settlement later, also the methods for excluding the Jews. A Programme of principles cannot be expected to be a Programme of action, giving tactical details of how supremacy is to be secured, etc. I am opposed altogether to fixing our Programme too rigidly, for in this great struggle we must first determine the principles from which we shall never draw back, and not imitate the vote-catching methods of the bourgeois and Socialist Parties.

Economic Policy

It is the duty of the National Government to provide the necessaries of life and not to secure the highest possible profits for Capital. It may occur to simple, plain-thinking men that to announce this obvious fact as a principle is superfluous. It is a common-place to the producer, the farmer, the artizan, the manufacturer, that what he makes is either used or consumed, — by himself or, as an article of commerce, by others. In his eyes business which is not concerned with production or consumption is ridiculous, impossible, and against common sense.

This brings us to one of the great intellectual difficulties in our recruiting work. Our fellow-countrymen are bound to say: — Of course your natural sentiment in thinking of the meanings and aims of labour and economics is quite correct, but unfortunately our so-called political economy of today in no way answers to this natural claim. If you look closer you will discover the terrible characteristics which are utterly opposed to the obvious duty of all national political economy. — For what about the money-lenders and profiteers? Do these universal plunderers

4. The Programme Requirements In Detail

give a thought to providing the necessaries of life? No! Are they engaged in creating values, do they produce anything? No! They are robbers and traitors in the economic sense, and merely amass wealth for themselves.

What about the banks? They circulate money and give 'credit'. Yes; but the Post Office does this, and cheaper, quicker and better; and to whom do the banks give credit? — To the needy, the labouring masses, who have no home of their own, or for building houses? No! Or to the farmers, or to those who run businesses and who produce and distribute the economic necessaries? Not freely, and only if security is offered, over and above the natural engagement to repay; moreover they charge interest. Do the banks care whether the producers' customers are served well, cheaply and promptly, or whether economic necessaries are supplied quickly, cheaply and with due attention? No! Their one thought is for making their profit out of the interest, commission, or whatever the banking process of tapping the supply of money is called. What do the banks produce? Nothing! What do they earn? Vast sums.

Thus money-lenders, profiteers, banks, financiers, supply no necessity, but instead they draw huge profits from the prevailing capitalist system, — in fact they tyrannise over and exploit the anti-social economic system of today. The main task of economics is to see that the interest on loans is secure, i. e. the workers are forced to give up part of their earnings to the 'City'. What does the factory-owner, or as the workers call him, the 'exploiter' and 'blood-sucker' do? By paying the lowest possible wages, by using inferior material, by mass-production, averaging, and high retail prices, he tries to make the largest possible profit for himself.

He gives no thought to his employees poverty; he does not care if his wares have to be quickly thrown away as rubbish, — all the better, since it means more work and more profits for him. The silly people rush again and again after cheap rubbish, as long as it is displayed attractively. The return on his capital comes first with him, supplying necessaries of life comes a bad second.

The true factory-owner is something quite different, he who is conscious of his high task as an economic leader. He must possess high moral worth — in the economic sense at least. His task is to discover the real economic needs of the people — if he is also an inventor he does this pioneer work himself. He must keep his costs as low as he can and lay them out to the best advantage, keep prices down as low as possible in order to get his goods on to the market; keep up both quality and quantity of production, pay his employees well, so that they may be able to purchase goods freely, must always be thinking of improvements and renewals of plant and trading methods. If he puts all this first in his business, he is 'supplying the necessaries of life' in the best and highest sense, ' and profits will come of themselves without his making them his first object. The finest and most universally known example of this kind of manufacturer is Henry Ford. There are other names in our own heavy industries which stand equally high, — Krupp, Kirdorf, Abbe, Mannesmann, Siemens, and numerous others.

The character of such businesses is altogether different when they are not personally controlled by men of high moral qualities who look after the interests of their workers, but are handed over to impersonal limited companies.

So long as the founder of a business is also the chief shareholder and can maintain the standard of excellence of his products, all may be well; but as soon as conversion takes place it is overwhelmed by the interests of the capitalist shareholders. The former owners, the managers, now depend on the Board, representing the share-holders, for improvements in business methods and working conditions, — and the shareholders have no interest (beyond that of the slave-driver) in the welfare of the workers and the excellence of the work, so long as the dividends coming out of it are good large ones. The introduction

4. The Programme Requirements In Detail

of proprietory shares has had a most devastating influence, for any chance speculator can corner the shares and actually become owner of large industrial works without knowing anything about them. To the Stock Exchange stocks and shares are merely so much paper for them to play with. They are not interested in conditions of production and labour, most of them could not say what the products or the conditions of marketing, labour, wages and maintenance are in the business of which they are the owners by law. (!) And owners they actually are, just because they happen to have cornered the shares of this or that factory in the market.

Let us now examine this state of affairs in the light of its effect on political economy, so as to realise the corrupt character of the capitalist system.

Today business merely looks for a return on capital. The large retail stores follow different methods. They cultivate 'attraction', 'bluff, 'averaging', 'luxury articles', and arouse desire for non-necessities, as I have shown above.

Great palaces, built with all the arts of refinement, invite to purchase apparently cheap, but mostly quite useless articles, and by offering easy conditions of payment they entice their customers to spend all manner of sums on pure luxury. Rest-rooms are provided to enable people to spend a long time in the stores, which thus become mere hotbeds for extravagance, for let no one imagine he gets anything as a present. Really well-off people don't buy in large stores; they know what the poorer one don't know — he who buys cheap buys dear. Do the crowds who buy in those palaces imagine that they were built otherwise than with their saved up pennies? Do they think they get off paying for the escalators, the lifts, the rest-rooms, the fairy-like illumination?

Realise, also, that the large stores spell ruin to the small shop-keepers, that they exploit home-labour and their staff most cruelly, that what is manufactured is mostly rubbish. The better articles are usually dearer than in respectable specialised shops, a fact which justifies our fight against the large stores. We regard them as a special form of the capitalistic idea in practical operation, which does not provide necessaries of life, but is merely there for the purpose of producing huge profits for the shareholders. Given this leading conception of provision of the necessaries of life (which, we should observe, has nothing to do with the Communist scheme of economics), the question ranks first in importance in our attitude towards private property.

8. National Socialism recognises private ownership of property as a principle and protects it by law, — given that it is acquired and employed honourably. We cannot discuss it here, but any one who rightly comprehends the term 'work' will quickly see that the product of 'work' must be the property of him who works. A producer will fail to understand why his work, or its value, should be the property of a vague 'community', nor will he readily admit that the fruits of his labour should go to an individual, the capitalist. Hence a right understanding of the meaning of 'work' leads naturally to recognition of private ownership.

There is finally a further subject — the conception of the home. The Home is not a reality unless it really is a man's own property, and his own home shelters his own family. A man's own fruit and vegetables out of his own garden taste better than a meal eaten in a crowded eating house. Any one who does not know the longing for possessions nor the joy of possession, will fail to understand the importance of recognising private ownership. Such a man has no roots anywhere. It is curious that the preying type of man is always envious, always seeking something fresh to possess, whilst the Nordic man, the solid man of the soil, is absolutely modest in his ideas. He wants no more than he can get by his work. A workman does not wish to have a fine villa which he could never earn; he wants a nice little house of his own, not a hired one for which in the course of his life he would

4. The Programme Requirements In Detail

be paying three or four times much as the house cost to build. But the Jew, the capitalist, — he does not want to be tied to any plot of land; his ideal is a big safe stuffed with scrip, mortgage deeds and promissory notes. Wealth, not in property but in other people's mortgaged property, is his aim. He does not work, but he rests not till he has amassed bundles of bonds giving him the whip hand over all those to whom he has lent money. The next demand of our Programme is framed in order to put a stop to this.

9. The welfare of the nation demands that a limit shall be set to the amassing of wealth in the hands of individuals.

Wealth is not injurious in itself; on the contrary, possessions well administered do good to all who are connected with them. But again it is the capitalist system of loans which has turned wealth from a blessing into a curse; it is robbery. The great mass of possessionless workers and the indebted middle class are getting further and further separated from the rich; countless small owners are distrained upon for debt, and the power of the financiers, who know no fatherland, no home-land, waxes ever more sinister, as they sit in their modern robber-baron castles, the banks. To meet this the National State shall see to it that:

10. All Germans shall be formed into a community of work for the furtherance of the common welfare and Kultur.

This idea of community of work implies the economic overthrow of the universalist conception of society. All work and production must be included within the higher idea of service to the community. It is in no way opposed to personal effort and industry, but it means that individual progress shall not be at the expense of one's fellow men.

11. Within the frame of the general duty of work attaching to every German, and with recognition of private ownership as a principle, every German shall be free to earn in whatever

manner he chooses, and free to dispose of the results of his labour.

The foregoing expressly rejects the socialising schemes of Marxism and also high finance. The State shall include the greatest possible number of free existences linked by the social idea of service. — It is of course out of the question to run mines, blast-furnaces, rolling mills, shipyards on a small scale, but a hundred thousand free and independent master-shoemakers are better than five monster shoe factories.

The great landed estates in the North and East of Germany are more productive by being run on a large scale than if managed by small freehold farmers. Small freeholds do best if within easy reach of towns and villages. Our No. 12 demands that:

12. A healthy combination of businesses of all kinds, large and small, including farming, shall be maintained.

13. Great businesses (syndicates, trusts) are nationalised. This demand is consistent with our general struggle against the capitalistic idea. — The first aim of syndicates and trusts in any particular branch of production is to unite with other similar businesses for the purpose of dictating prices. They are governed by no desire to distribute good wares at a cheap price. Such 'rings' are specially attracted by new businesses which are doing well. New firms in the same line of business are bought up and put out of the way, often at a very large price by way of compensation. Supply is regulated by pooling, by which means they are able to regulate prices in accordance with an apparently genuine 'supply and demand'. That is what concerns the shareholders, who have no desire to see prices kept low by competition. New ideas and inventions are viewed with a hostile eye,' and preferably suppressed if their adoption would endanger the paying capacity of older plants. Such businesses, run as huge trusts from a big central office, are clearly 'ripe for socialisation', i.e. they have

4. The Programme Requirements In Detail

ceased to fulfil any of the services to the community which individual competition performs. They are paralysed from the start and only serve the greed of capitalism.

14. Usurers and profiteers, and ruthless self-enrichment at the expense of the nation, shall be punished with death.

The Law, as it is now, gives special protection to individual property. Small thefts are punished inhumanly, whereas the Law supplies no way of catching large scale swindlers, who rob an entire nation by 'capitalistic methods'. We refer especially to those who promoted and profited by the inflation. It was the first time in history that an entire industrious nation was robbed of the whole of its savings by a crime of inflation on the vast scale as happened in Germany.

The greed of the banks after the stabilisation was worse than highway robbery. More Germans fell victims to the practices of the 'war companies' than to any organised robber band. When the time comes we shall deal with these things more in detail, and shall have to find a legal formula for them. But everyone will agree that 'organised fraud against the nation' must be punished as, and even more, severely than small thefts of money, or fraud.

15. Introduction of an obligational year of labour or service for every German.

The obligation to serve by working will be the visible expression to the public of the duty of service. It is meant to be educational, and to place before each German an example of the whole community working as one man together. It will show to each German the blessing of the strict fulfilment of duty in working for the service of the nation.

The Programme of the N.S.D.A.P.

Financial Policy - Breaking the Thraldom of Interest

Our principles on this subject have been so fully set down in the second chapter, that we shall only describe here the measures suitable for achieving our objective in practice.

16. Liberation of the State, and so of the nation, from its indebtedness and from the obligation to pay interest to the great financial houses. The State may make no debts — for it has no necessity to do so.

There is no comparison between the State and the private person who every now and then requires loans and is forced to make debts. The State controls the Mint; it can thus make money, which the private person cannot do! It did this in a lunatic fashion during the periods of inflation. It did the same with the Rentenmark, and the same — after resigning its control to the so-called Reichsbank — with the so-called Reichsmark.

The State could make far better use of this right to make money, without the danger of inflation being involved. — But only if first:

17. The Reichsbank and all the issuing banks are nationalised, and,

18. If there is provision of money for all great public services (water-power, railroads, etc.) not by means of loans, but by granting non-interest-bearing State bonds, without using ready money.

In other words: — Wanton printing of bank notes, without creating new values, means inflation. We all lived through it. But the correct conclusion is that an issue of non - interest - bearing bonds by the State cannot produce inflation if new values are at the same time created.

The fact that today great economic enterprises cannot be set on

4. The Programme Requirements In Detail

a sound footing without recourse to loans is sheer lunacy. Here is where reasonable use of the State's right to produce money which might produce the most beneficial results.

It must be clear to anyone that, for instance, a great electrical plant using water-power might well be erected in the following unexceptional manner:

The Government introduces a Bill in the legislative Council for exploiting the water-power of Bavaria, Saxony, etc., by satisfying all economic requirements. The local Diet, or other body, decides on construction, empowers the Finance Minister or the State Bank to issue a series of banknotes, marked specially to show that they are fully covered by the new works under contemplation. These notes are supported by the combined credit of the State or the Reich. No one can show any objection on the score of inflation. Construction takes place on the additional credit granted by the Council representing the nation, and the notes become legal tender like the rest.

When the work is completed, electricity is supplied to customers against this money, and in a few years the issue can be recalled and destroyed. Result: The State, the nation has instituted a new work, which secures to them a great new source of revenue, and the nation is the richer by it. To prove the folly of the present system let us compare the foregoing with what goes on now.

A loan is taken up. A few capitalists do what the whole nation, even though Parliament may vote in favour of it, cannot do; they allow the State to borrow money from them. Instead of using its direct authority for the benefit of the nation, the State engages to pay permanent interest for the sum required to complete certain work, thereby hanging a mill-stone round its neck. And, what is most costly of all, it issues bonds thus creating 'fresh purchasing capacity'. On the balance-sheet it makes no difference whether the new work is represented by new paper money or new bonds. But the community suffers injury because the bonds imply that the new work is mortgaged to capital, which naturally makes itself quite secure, dictates prices, and takes the profits. Thus it is really the financiers who are the richer by the development of the nation's water-power; they are indifferent about repayment; they like to have to such monopolies as permanent milking cows. The population are forced to pay dear for electricity, and once again a part of the national property is converted in the interests of the financiers.

I must refer the reader to my earlier writings, especially Der deutsche Staat, which treats these questions in more detail than is possible in this pamphlet. Several numbers in this series, moreover, deal with various special aspects of the coming State's novel methods of creating money.

19. Demands the introduction of a fixed standard of coinage. That we admittedly have now, but the robbery remains the same as before. We National Socialists have everything ready, once we are in power, for bringing the inflation swindle to an end forthwith, and for introducing a new guaranteed standard of coinage.

20. Establishment of a new national bank for the development of the economy.

This demand is exhaustively explained in Pamphlet 8 of the National Socialist Library: Die Wohnungsnotund die Sociale Bau-und Wirtschaftsbank als Retterin aus Wohnung selend, Wirtschaftskrise und Erwerbslosenelend. It is remarkable that this demand of ours for a financial policy has penetrated deeply into other political circles besides our own. In 1921 I submitted this demand to the Bavarian Government in the form of a fully worked out Bill. There was at first much sympathy with the idea: but once the 'experts' — banking fraternity — were drawn into consultation, the Government rejected 'Feder's Utopia'.

After the successful Election in Thuringia in February, 1924, our Party in the Landtag there worked hard for establishing such a

4. The Programme Requirements In Detail

bank and found von Klüchtzner, the Finance Minister, prepared to co-operate; the bourgeois section also were in sympathy. By a majority vote in the Landtag the Government were empowered to establish a Social Bank for development and economy. Whereupon the Government of the Reich, under pressure from the Reichsbank, forbade the will of the people being carried out.

I had in the meanwhile managed to have a Bill in outline introduced in the Reichstag, providing for similar banks in the different States; in the short Session of the Dawes year (1924) however, it was cautiously postponed by the Government Parties until the dissolution in the autumn of that year.

A Bill for a bank was before the Landtag of Mechlenburg. The Resolution was made ineffective by the vacillation of the German-nationalist Finance Minister, also owing to the obstacles which the Reichsbank was expected to place in the way.

The idea underlying the bank for development is no less simple than the plan explained above for creating money for great public purposes.

A combined economic corporation, such as the bank for economic development, should be given the right to issue money for development (Baumark - Scheinen) covered by the value of the newly built houses. These could then be erected free from the huge burden of interest, which alone today makes it impossible to build in sufficient quantities.

Every German with a home of his own. A free people on unencumbered land.

21. Complete re-modelling of the system of taxation on social political economic principles. Delivery of the consumer from the burden of indirect taxation, and the producer from taxes which cramp his activities.

Social Policy

Social policy is the favorite motto of our present political cure-alls. It sounds so nice, makes them popular, and attracts votes for the Party which promises to make everything right.

When every Party promises the official, for instance, an increase of pay, they call that Social Policy.

It is the same when they promise to grant the wishes of the clerks and workers; or when they do a little to relieve people with small incomes, or war sufferers, or young teachers, or Germans abroad. .And all the people run after these political rat-catchers when they play on their 'social' flute.[26] It must first be made clear that Social Policy denotes, The public welfare the highest law, and that, as now understood, Social policy is really one of self-interest having no regard to the general welfare. All sorts of careless promises are made, and those who make them must know from the start that it is impossible to fulfil them.

Now that Germany is so powerless politically, economically and financially, — which finds expression first in the Dawes Laws and now in the Young Law, and in the so-called policy of fulfilment which has laid burdens on our nation, making life almost impossible — it is both false and ridiculous to talk about 'Social Policy'. Now that German life is so cramped, when each man is treading on his neighbour and trying to get ahead of him and to shove him aside, when the different classes of the population are at variance, promises to favour one group at the expense of another are not 'Social Policy for the general good', but one of inciting one class against another. They know very well that a momentary 'improvement' is annulled by a higher cost of living and higher taxation.

Social policy means something very different — a determination to solve the social problem.

---

26   An allusion to the "Pied Piper" of Hamelin

4. The Programme Requirements In Detail

The out-of-luck, the exploited working classes believe that their just wages, their proper position in the social order is being withheld from them — hence class war.

It is clear to all that our economic life is suffering from deep injuries, bitter injustice. And yet the conclusions drawn by Marxism with its 'class war' and its 'social and economic demands' of 'expropriating the expropriator' and 'socialisation' are utterly false, for that strikes at all the true requirements of a genuine social policy, whose highest law is the general welfare.

The leading principle of class war — as a principle of policy — is hatred. 'Expropriation of the expropriator' makes of envy a principle of economics, and 'socialisation' means striking down personality in leadership, and setting up materialism, the mass, in the place of intellect and efficiency.

Nothing further is needed to prove the utter break-down of the Marxist doctrines, seeing the complete bankruptcy of the Communist system of economics and the miserable failure of the German Revolution of 1918.

I would call my readers' particular attention to the fact that this pseudo-socialism, born of Marxism, is not founded on common sense nor on any 'social' idea, is not constructive, but remains sunk in the lowest depths of political thought, that it rests on the same general principle of crass and chaotic individualism as we have always known it to do. It is believed merely by a number of individuals, united by feelings of hatred and envy — not by any constructive purpose — against the other half of the nation. Can we be surprised that the social question is not, and cannot be, solved by this means, and that their sole solution is hatred and the desire for loot; that a living State could not result from the Marxist Stock Exchange revolt, but only a heap of ruins.

Once again National Socialism finds the right word: Stock Exchange revolt. Marxism is an expression of capitalistic treason.

Capitalistic, because when a society founded on individualism has fallen into chaos, it of necessity falls under the sway of the great financial magnate.

The social-political theories, which pretend to be 'anti-capitalistic' (Marxism, the war between classes) — Social policy as understood today — are necessarily capitalistic, for they share the same intellectual principle. They have not the wish to construct organically member by member, to interlock with painful care the different classes working under the high conception of national unity, but their aspirations are purely selfish, their wish is to better their own position without regard to others.

Capitalism and Marxism are one and the same! They grow on the same intellectual stem. There is a whole world of difference between them and us, their bitterest opponents. Our whole conception of the construction of society differs widely from theirs. It is neither a class-struggle nor class-selfishness, but — our chief law is the general welfare

22. Great developments in Old Age Insurance by nationalising life - annuities. Every member of the German nation shall be assured of enough to live upon on attaining a certain age, and before that age if permanently disabled.

That is the solution of the social problem.

It is not so much direct discontent with wages, salaries and incomes which causes social tension, as uncertainty, a man's anxiety about his later years, lest he may be flung on the streets. It is this knawing anxiety which drives the various occupations to join together in sham-social organisations of the Marxist and capitalist types and embitters the animosity between employer and employee. It releases the basest instincts on both sides, and mutual animosity is the result. The worker's proper aim in life fades away in the struggle for a momentary increase of wages,

4. The Programme Requirements In Detail

and he never realises that the great aim of social policy should be the proper provision for old age.

We note once again how the State discovered a good and commendable solution in the case of the official class, by providing for them after retirement. It is the proper and happy solution of the capitalist ideal of income, namely to convert it into the true State's ideal of provision, based on personal labour and efficiency.

It will be the highest and noblest aim of National Socialism to realise this standard of general welfare.

23. Profit-sharing for all.

The N.S.D.A.P. identifies itself with this demand. It is in fact a purely socialist demand in the proper sense of the word; nevertheless it comes to us as an attractive but corrupting present from capitalism.

Sharing of profits arising out of the work of others comes under the heading of "unearned income" which is most sharply attacked by National Socialism. However, a man sharing the profits from his own labour is a demand so natural and socially so just, that nothing can be advanced against it as a principle.

It is in the carrying of it out that the difficulty arises, that is, in limiting the amount of the share due to the production, skill and industry of the worker, and of that due to the brainwork of the inventor, the accountant, the merchant, the management, and other circumstances connected with the business.

It is of course highly important that the parties who increase the value of a product should not be left out of consideration. Even under the present system some part of the booty which capital hopes to get out of a business could be recovered for the worker.

The Programme of the N.S.D.A.P.

We shall not discuss here the question of how later on the National Socialist State will solve the problem.

I personally considered that a general lowering of prices, at the same time maintaining wages at the present level, would be the better and more practical way to fulfil the demand for sharing out the profits of the whole of our national production.

It is however possible that the National Socialist State will solve the problem in a far more comprehensive manner than is conceived today by brains with a Marxist and capitalistic tendency. The present demand for profit-sharing springs either from a desire for profits (essentially capitalistic), or from envy (essentially Marxist).

In the ideal State alone, as we conceive it, is it justified, because, when we come to solve it, we must avoid the capitalistic method of granting a small share in the business, the sole object of which is to secure for the larger shareholders their right to their dividends, and also the Marxist idea of envy, for that debases the personal factor and injures the general public.

We give a few examples for the sake of clarity.

It does no good to the 'profit-sharing' workers in a shoe factory to get a few shares in the business or a small bonus or a pair of shoes at cost price, if they have to pay just as dear for their shirts, suits, socks, food and drink, because the tailors, bakers and brewers cover the greed of the clothiers, bakeries and breweries by their own 'profit-sharing'.

Lowering of prices is the charm which must give every member of the nation a share in the profits of national production.

It will not satisfy the feeling of social justice of a genuine National Socialist if the street-sweepers, day-labourers, railway-men, postmen, transport-workers, hospital-workers —

4. The Programme Requirements In Detail

to name only a few —, agricultural labourers, miners, builders' labourers, are to be excluded from profit-sharing, simply because these classes do not contribute to increase values. Also of agriculture, (in which not merely the details of farming have to be considered, but also the millions engaged in other businesses connected with it) it must be said that it 'pays' in years when the harvest is good; in the heavy industries also, the mines only yield a bare profit owing the pressure of world competition.

Can we assert that these millions of workers and employees, who are often engaged in most important branches of industry, but who, owing to the circumstances, cannot hope for a direct share in the profits, are to get less consideration than the numerous class, who work perhaps as washers-up or porters in a nightclub or a Turkish bath, or in an optical or chemical factory enjoying a monopoly and supplying the whole world? Are the latter to share the profits and dividends on luxury production, are they to make it more and more impossible for the majority of the nation to attain to these advantages?

We like to contemplate a shower of dividends, bonuses, Christmas presents of money poured out upon workers and officials, who have done splendid work for a business for years. Such aspirations of a social-political nature need not be discussed and argued in this treatise on general principles. The demand, as things are now, is an important demand, and one which should attract adherents. 'Profits' depend mainly on the general business situation and on the technical skill and salesmanship of the management; failure may come through faulty construction or a mistake in calculations. However skilled the workers may be, however industrious, they can have little or no influence on the results of the year's work, or on the gains or losses. Their efficiency justifies them in demanding a proper and sufficient wage, but there are no moral or economic grounds for their claiming a share in the profits. They would quite rightly resist the suggestion that they should cover any losses of the business year out of their savings; they would rightly resist being expected to make up, by a lowering of wages, for bad management or extravagant living on the part of the directors. But 'profit-sharing' is only justifiable if there is ability and readiness to share risks and losses, or if special effcency merits it". Here is one aspect of general profit-sharing.

Why, for instance, should the great dye-works of Germany, with their predominant position of monopoly, continue to be but a capitalistic milking cow for the shareholders of the I. G. Farbenindustrie, and at the best, by raising prices, give a share of profits to their workers and officials?

It will be the task of the National Socialist State to see that huge monopolist profits shall be placed at the general disposal by a most generous lowering of prices.

It is obvious that the problem is not a question of Social policy, but is closely bound up with the present-day capitalistic social order (shareholders's claims).

We wish to apply these shortly expressed principles; and to be guided by them in our aim of realising profit-sharing as widely as possible in all businesses in which the profits go exclusively into the pockets of professional financiers.

24. Expropriation of all profits not made by honest work, but through the war, the Revolution — and further — the stabilisation and re-valuation of the mark; also the property of money-lenders and grabbers.

This is a measure of punishment and justice, requiring no explanation under any principle.

25. Removal of the shortage of housing by extensive building throughout the Reich with the means provided under No. 20 (the bank for development). This closes the list of social-

4. The Programme Requirements In Detail

political demands. On the technical financial question not much can be said in this pamphlet, for it is a very large special subject, and one which, it would seem, only financial minds understand and which actually will have to be carried out by them.

Religion and Art

It is not possible to state on this subject more than a very few leading principles in the space of a programme. That has already been done. For the rest it must be our principle not to drag questions of religion into statements on general politics; although we may well treat the corrupting influence of the secret doctrines of Judaism as an object for public statements and attacks.

The same applies to all foolish attacks on Christianity. Expressions such as "Christianity has only done harm" merely show that the man who says them has neither human nor political intelligence.

One may well blame the Church for meddling in politics, and all good Christians will disapprove of the cruelties practiced in the name of the Cross by the Inquisition and trials for witchcraft, but it is wrong to abuse in general terms the greatest phenomenon in human history for the mistakes and depravities of individuals. The Christian religion has raised and edified millions and millions and brought them to God by the way of suffering.

The culture of the Middle Ages stood up in the sign of the Cross; achievement, sacrifice, courageous faith have their roots in Christianity. Thus we must be careful to distinguish the inner spiritual kernel of Christianity from the various forms of excrescence which have appeared upon it in its passage through history.

Our Party stands upon the basis of positive Christianity.

This is not the place to discuss all the problems, hopes and desires as to whether the German nation may at some time discover some new form for its religious beliefs and experiences; these are matters quite beyond the limits of a Programme such as that of National Socialism.

It is of urgent importance to set our face against all the disruptive influences which are doing harm to our nation in the domain of art, literature, science, the stage, the moving pictures, and above all throughout the entire Press. Our Programme of principles — the 25 Points — goes far enough into detail for it to be unnecessary to say any more on this subject.

Military and Other Reforms

The national Army, the Chambers of trades and professions, reform of the franchise and the law, are such vast questions affecting public: life, that they cannot be dealt with in a few sentences. The leading ideas are set out in the Programme itself, but the task of thinking and working them out and, above all, of grafting them on to the historical past will be the great problem of the coming years, when we hope that political power will be ours, and when we shall have be equipped with the force and knowledge necessary for taking over the business of the State.

Here we have a rich field for research under National Socialism. The significance of National Socialism is shown by the fact that it leaves no domain of the national life untouched; for it provides an entirely new foundation on which we shall have to build up that life.

5. What We Do Not Desire

In order to strengthen the positive side of our Programme it will be well to state shortly what we do not desire.

We do not desire the wheels of history to turn backwards nor to restore to life dynasties which faded away, leaving hardly a trace of themselves — through their own fault. Nor do we desire to set the classes that have been dethroned up again in their former privileged positions. The officer class and the officials are really no higher or better than any other professional class, in so far as they genuinely work in with our idea of serving the nation first of all. It is not a uniform or gold lace, but performance, which make a man.

We do not desire one-sided preference or artificial elevation for the working class, nor any kind of proletarian dictatorship. No man may talk himself into believing that any class may, simply from having been oppressed in the past, assume a claim to be given power. Such aspirations, when translated into realities, unfailingly lead to terrible consequences, such as those which accompanied the Stock Exchange revolt of November, 1918. So far it is not the 'oppressed' section of the population which are on top, but a crowd of political swindlers, greedy adventurers, profiteers, jabberers and fools, who have got possession of the political machine and the administration. The promised dictatorship of the proletariat has turned into

The Dictatorship of the 'Profitariat'

Even a new ordering of the State under National Socialism could have no hope of success unless it had at its disposal a very thoroughly trained staff of resolute men completely imbued with the principles of our Programme, serious men of energy and experience. Even with us too many pure demagogues would elbow their way in and reap advantage under the new order.

It is much easier to criticise the faults of a collapsing social order than to do constructive work on it.

We require not merely a new Party, slowly obtaining a footing in Parliament and administration, and then perhaps accepting a post or two in a coalition Ministry, only to get its back broken in the end, — for then our part in history would be played out, just as today Social Democracy is finished as a political and intellectual force in Germany. The same applies to the German Nationalists, who have already gone back on their main principles in order to get seats in the Government.

We do not want Ministers who take office purely for the sake of the position or for power, but we shall consider any such position as a stage towards our great objective. Between ourselves and the rest there is always the flaming sword of our world theory.

On the one side the State, or rather the sham State, of the Liberal-democratic-parliamentary stamp, forced by necessity to mask the tyranny of the financiers, and at its feet a seething mob of Jew camp-followers and place-hunters, fighting to make a living out of the system.

On our side, the fight for the liberation and purification of our people, till we achieve the true State of social justice and national liberty.

6. Conclusion

The task of this first pamphlet of the N.S. Library is to teach the National Socialist what he should know about the Party Programme. We have seen again and again the single main principle which is drawn through all our arguments like a scarlet thread: National Socialism is a theory of the world, standing in sharp opposition to the present-day world of capitalism and its Marxist and bourgeois satellites.

Our life is a struggle in the service of this mighty idea, a struggle for a new Germany.

We National Socialists wave our storm-banner before the world. Ever young, shining and glittering in the sun, rises the Hooked Cross, the symbol of re-awakening life.

www.ingramcontent.com/pod-product-compliance
Lightning Source LLC
Chambersburg PA
CBHW072202160426
43197CB00012B/2493